...an Basha gloriosissime Reportata 22 Iunÿ 1593

PETRINIA

DRENZIHNA

ENIA

Text by STANE STANIČ

A Motovun Group Book

© APROS & APROS Ltd 1998

Published by FLINT RIVER PRESS
London 1995
Revised by APROS & APROST
LJUBLJANA 1999

ISBN: 1 871489 18 0

Design:
Gane Aleksic

Editors:
Nada Jane Kronja
Madge Phillips

Translation:
Klara Stanič
S.P. Stone
Ian Wraight

Colour separation by
Grafika, Ilirska Bistrica

Printed and bound by
Editoriale Lloyd, Trieste

CONTENTS

25
TOO EARLY OR TOO LATE?
From Austria-Hungary via Yugoslavia to independence

52
OUT OF THE SEA OF TETHYS
Geography. The creation of the land. The Karst.

90
THE REVOLVING DOOR OF EUROPE
Routes ancient and modern. Prehistory.
Illyrians, Celts and Romans.

96
THE MIRACLE UNDER TRIGLAV
Slovene origins and settlement. Samo's Karantania.
The Dark Ages. Baptism by the Savica.

117
THE DARKNESS OF THE NEW DAWN
Under the Frankish feudal yoke. Christianity and literacy.
Enthronement of the Karantanian dukes.
Germanic settlement. Death and destruction.

158
WAITING FOR KING MATJAŽ
Ottoman conquests. Turkish raids. Peasant rebellions.
Protestantism and Counter-reformation.
The mythical monarch.

183
MATJAŽ IS NOT COMING
Mining, industry and trade. Enlightenment and Absolutism.
Napoleon and the Illyrian Provinces.
National Awakening.

242
AND WHAT ABOUT TOMORROW?
The struggle for independence. Population.
Literature, arts and architecture. Slovene emigration.
Economic trends. The national character.

284
CHRONOLOGY

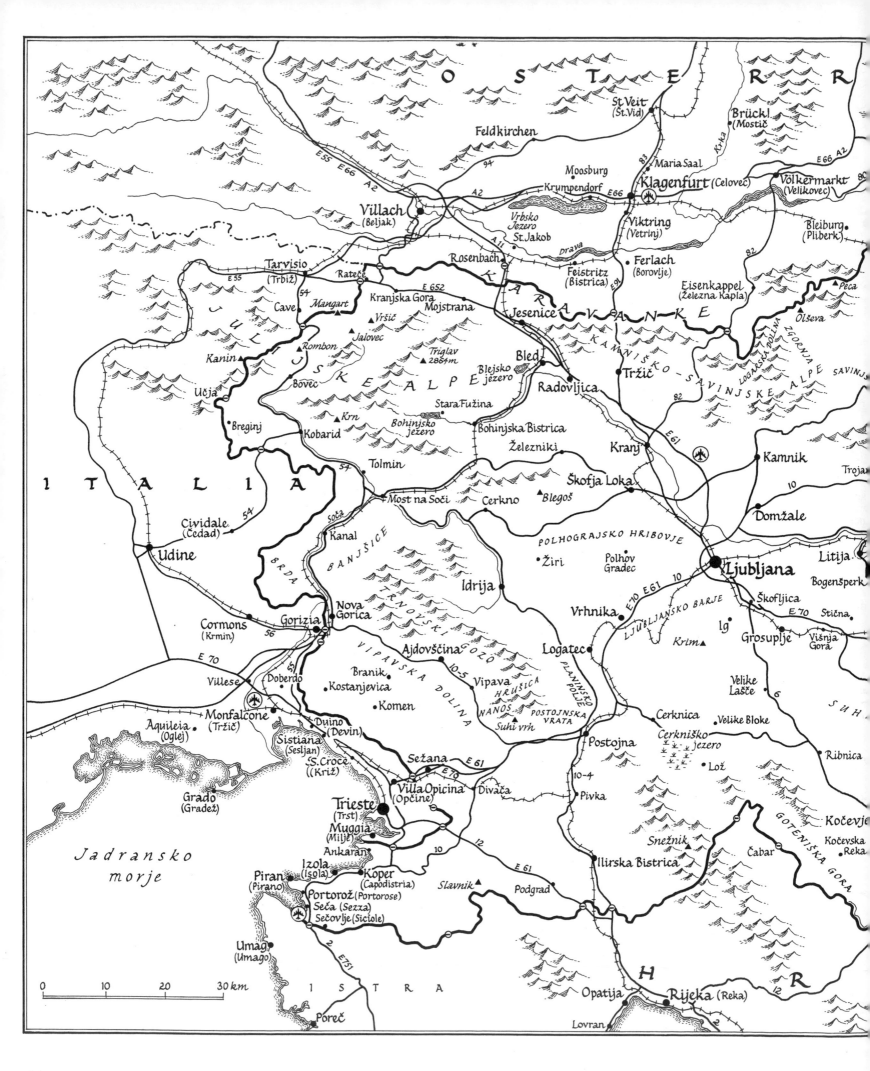

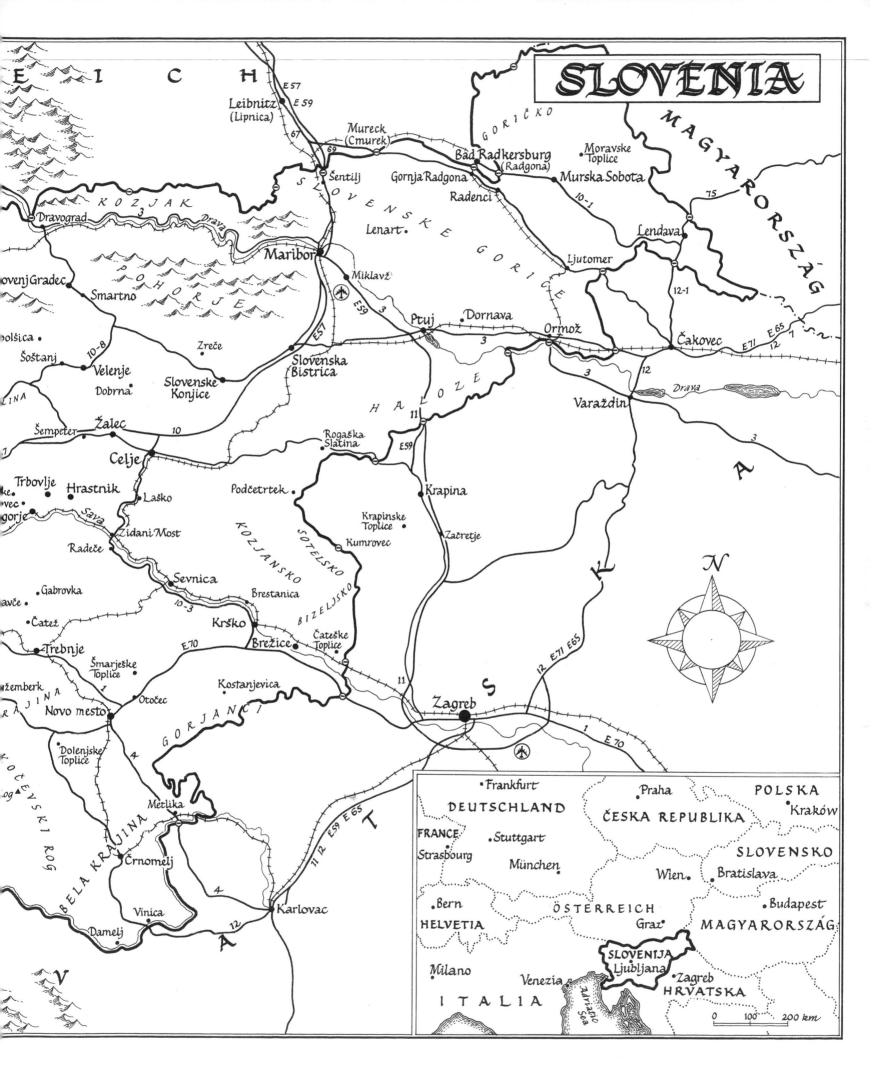

SLOVENIA

INTRODUCTION

SLOVENIA STEPPED ONTO THE WORLD STAGE only a decade before the start of the Third Millennium. Nestled in their small corner of the heart of Europe, it took the Slovenes almost fifteen centuries to finally achieve their own sovereign and independent state.

After the Second World War, Slovenia had become one of the six republics making up the Socialist Federal Republic of Yugoslavia. When it later entered a claim for a place of its own amongst the nations of the world, it encountered a tendency in Europe and beyond to dismiss the formation of new states and small countries as anachronistic in today's day. "Common sense" was inclined against the 'revival of nationalistic relics of a bygone century', and the 'folkloric outpourings of provincial patriots'. For quite a few people the whole exercise seemed simply in poor taste.

The appearance of so many new states on Europe's political map near the very end of the Twentieth Century is often taken as a sign of disintegration or dissolution. For some people it is all a bit déjà vu it recalls the rise of Denmark, Norway and Finland, and the process of Scandinavianisation. Others are more disparaging and prefer to call it Balkanisation. When the recent events in the former-Yugoslavia are designated secessionism an admonishing finger is usually raised, for the turning of the new millennium is the era of European inter-linking and integration. These are supposed to be times of global technological and political integration, not fragmentation.

So where did the Slovenes' drive and determination to become independent come from after seventy years of living in not just one but two communal Yugoslavias? Why were they so adamant about it that they were even prepared to take up arms to gain it? What does the Slovenia of today have to say about itself and its long journey towards statehood?

These and other questions are considered by the author in recounting the past and present of his country, the evolution of the life and customs of the Slovenes down many centuries, always in the shadow of powerful neighbours.

3. Different places, different ways. A young lady may coquettishly use the flowers on her window-sill as a shield from curious eyes, or perhaps, as an invitation to enter. Or perhaps both at the same time.

4.　　...but whichever way - the usual epilogue, is a white bouquet.

5. The Lenten Carnival and the advancing spring usually do their part. That is what masks are for. This one helps chase away the winter in the best of pagan traditions. Of course the lucky couple in the preceding picture have nothing to do with masks anymore. They let them fall before starting out on their conjugal life.

6. The old train takes us back through time in one part of the country, chugging past gleaming modern factories and research centres and post-modern architecture as well as ancient churches, barns and bridges. Slovenia is aptly described as 'Europe's Oasis' Since each of its regions are so distinctive, it is actually more like a collection of oases

7. In the ecologically pristine country Slovenia aspires to become, every potential polluter will be served notice. But will gourmets forego their charcoal grills? Deep in the dense forests that cover more than one million hectares, wood is often still charred in the old traditional way.

8. To fill your basket you must first have one. Many diligent hands are leaving the factory machines and returning to the arts and crafts of yesteryear.

9. Knitting techniques vary from one part of the country to another, but not as much as the patterns do. Since prehistoric times, when the pile-dwellers of the Ljubljana Marshes decorated their urns, patterns have been important marks of distinction.

10. Laughing over stories of past foolishness is the stuff of spirited people with their unforgettable anecdotes.

11, 12. The wheel may have been a crucial disco-very for mankind, but today it is almost as great a discovery to find a traditional wheel-maker or wainwright. Wooden carts have in most places given way to tractors. Much less rare are the small dairies where farmers make their own cheese.

19

13.-15. The shiny new pull-cart adds new glints to the patina of the rustic backyard. The tantalising smell of bread freshly baked in the old wall ovens is pervasive. The door-posts of a zidanica, a hut in a vineyard, support many a dream of the grape-harvest.

16.-18. Enterprising souls fill their cellars with the traditional hams - well known for their unmatched taste and aroma. The farmer still tends his few sheep by hand; and takes his own wheat to the mill to make sure the flour is exactly to his taste.

19. Agriculture employs four tenths of Slovenia's population, and trends are downwards so this proportion will shrink further. Many who have left the land still treasure the costumes worn on festive occasions by their peasant ancestors.

20. Many family albums contain pictures of the demonstrations against the Yugoslav army and its attempts to block the process of democratization. In 1991 the Slovenian emblem took the place of the red star on the national flag.

21. In the new age, political meetings have given way to innumerable festivals and parades. This flower festival in Laško is accompanied by various entertainments and, since the town has an old and renowned brewery, naturally a certain amount of beer-drinking.

22. The 2864 m high Mt. Triglav is the highest in the country. The distinctive contours of its triple peaks was a symbol of the resistance in the Second World War, and now it is part of the national emblem. Innumerable songs and poems have been dedicated to it down the centuries. The strenuous climb to the top of Mt. Triglav has now become a patriotic must, sometimes in great force such as at the annual 'One Hundred Women on Triglav' or the 'Top on Top' climb that musters leading politicians and dignitaries. The rocky summit is becoming a cult site of sorts.

A YEARNING FOR INDEPENDENCE had been fermenting like yeast amongst the Slovenes even before the dawn of the Austro-Hungarian Empire soon enveloped them for more than a thousand years until its painful collapse in 1918. The Slovenes had lost their own 'kingdom' back in the Seventh Century and were scattered among a number of secular and ecclesiastical feudal estates states. They were bound together only by their ancient language, the linchpin of their cultural identity.

In the early Nineteenth Century Napoleon's battalions carried the spirit of the French Revolution to these lands and established the Illyrian Provinces. But the Illyrian Movement that followed in its wake did not entice the Slovenes to join with other 'Illyrians', as some other southern Slav and ethnic groups in the Balkans were often called at that time. Instead, they drew up their own national programme for a United Slovenia, just like the Italians, Czechs, Germans, Hungarians, Poles, Croats and others involved in the 1848 Spring of National Movements. All Slovenes under Austro-Hungarian rule would be united in their own Kingdom of Slovenia, with its own language, government, parliament and schools.

Forceful steps were taken to stop the ferment spreading through the Empire, but the Slovene Movement gained in strength. Mass assemblies were held in Slovenia Proper, and manifold ties were set up across into neighbouring lands. A pan-Slav movement was launched in Prague on 1 May 1848, with an appeal to all 'Slav brothers… to meet and reach an accord on a common platform at a Slav Congress'. This naturally called forth strong opposition from German and Hungarian political circles. The Austro-Hungarian Emperor soon resorted to a decree of absolute rule and set about quashing, all secessionist aspirations. But the bans were eased in 1861 and the patriotic movement quickly took wing again.

During the 1860s ties were forged with a group of Croatian politicians from Sisak. The Slovenes convened the 'First Yugoslav Congress' in Ljubljana on. 1-3 December 1870. It was the first of its kind in the history of the Southern Slav people. It gathered representatives of all the Southern Slavs in the Empire with the goal of 'uniting moral and material forces within the borders of the Habsburg Empire'. It sent a message of 'Austrian Slav' support to Serbian and Montenegrin brethren across the border who had already attracted the support of the Russianss.

This call for unity did not produce any strong response because it was so politically risky at the time and, more importantly, because the Southern Slav groups had different notions of equality. The bid for union was clearly premature. Only decades later, after the First World War had changed circumstances profoundly, did the 1848 programme become an option.

Austria-Hungary's military defeat in the First World War meant a long stride towards freedom. Before the war had ended an independent State of Slovenes, Croats and Serbs had been proclaimed by the Southern Slavs living inside the Empire. With great ceremony its founding charter was simultaneously signed in Ljubljana and Zagreb in Croatia on 29 October 1918. This new republic, which had both federal and confederal attributes, was proclaimed a full two weeks before Germany and Austria-Hungary formally capitulated and, it is worth noting, three days before combined Serbian and Entente forces liberated Belgrade, the Serbian capital, after they had breached the Thessalonika front.

The first Yugoslavia was weak and wobbly and its tribulations foreshadowed a series of later tragedies through to the present day. At the time of the formation of this new common state no one could foresee let alone weigh all the cohesive and disintegrative forces of the indigenous and foreign ingredients that were combined in the new country.

Naturally the former rulers of these lands, settled by the Slovenes for more than a thousand years, still wanted to retain control after World War I. France, which set store by the 'brotherhood-in-arms' it had forged with Serbia during the war, had strong interests in the area. So, too, did Great Britain and the United States of America. On its part, Italy reckoned that because it had changed sides and joined the Entente forces in the course of the war, and had the secret London Pact signed and sealed in its pocket, it could claim a handy slice of Balkan territories.

At the time Russia was virtually absent from the scene, fully preoccupied with its revolution at home. The United States of America might well have exercised a powerful influence on events, in view of its strong declaration that 'the world must be made safe for democracy'. But domestic pressures quickly turned it away from European affairs. Consequently the field was left wide open, for France in particular. From the outset it was clear that neither it nor Great Britain favoured a Yugoslav state of equal nations and preferred instead to support an expanded Serbia with its proven fidelity and loyal dynasty. Croats and Slovenes were suspected of being 'susceptible' to German influence.

THE SLOVENES WERE TOTALLY UNPREPARED for the 'coup' that was engineered at the end of 1918. A Serbian monarchy was simply foisted upon them in place of the federal republic they had intended. How could they, and the Croatian republicans aligned with them have been 'tricked so perfidiously' by Belgrade? Subsequently, during the between-wars period, accusations that the Slovene leaders had been naive and political dunces were hurled about. Undoubtedly, these criticisms really had other domestic political ends. Nevertheless, it is a truism that real statesmen do not let themselves be carried away by romantic dreams.

Slovenia's greatest and only true ally through that crucial period was US President Woodrow Wilson. Early in 1918 he presented a fourteen-point 'peace plan', which made room for the autonomous development of all the nations of the former Austro-Hungarian Empire. In a message to the US Congress a month later, he re-asserted the right of small nations to self-determination and warned that no one should tamper with it. These words emboldened the Slovenes and the liberation movement that had gotten under way after the Declaration of May 1917 by Slovene, Czech and Ruthenian delegations in the Vienna Parliament. The aim was to unite all the lands settled by Slovenes, Croats and Serbs, that had previously been ruled by the Habsburg dynasty into 'one independent corpus based on democratic foundations and free of all foreign domination'.

With enthusiastic popular support, in September 1918 a National Council of Slovenes, Croats and Serbs was founded as the supreme political representative of all the Southern Slavs living within the Austro-Hungarian Empire. Its ultimate goal was their unification in a single, free state. The 'Croat-Serb Coalition' from Croatia joined the Council bringing along its pro-Serbia faction despite the fact that this faction had always been opposed to the Council and had strong 'Greater Serbia' leanings.

Events unfolded rapidly. By the middle of October 1918, Emperor Charles pre-emptively tried issuing a manifesto promising to reorganise Austria as a federal state 'in which each national group will achieve its own statehood on the territory on which it lives'. The Palace in Vienna thus acquiesced to a trilateral solution granting equality with the Austrian Germans and the Hungarians to the Slav peoples who were the most numerous in the Empire.

In Slovenia, a Catholic priest and politician, Dr Anton Korošec was the most prominent figure in a movement which had advocated gradual independence within the Austria-Hungary framework. Even so, for some months before an audience with Emperor Charles in October 1918, Dr Korošec carefully eschewed every mention of the term 'Habsburg rule' which had still been used tactically in the May Declaration. He was keeping a careful eye on developments on the battle-front. The goal was becoming more and more clear-cut: to get out of that unloved monarchy post haste!

When the audience was finally held, the Emperor is said to have implored the Slovenes to remain loyal to the crown and the state. But Korošec was steadfast: 'Majestaet, es ist zu spaet!' ('Your Majesty, it is too late!') The audience came to a sad close, with the Emperor covering his eyes and sobbing, at least as far as the story goes.

SLOVENIA WOULD NEVER HAVE COME INTO BEING without the political perseverance of the Slovenes after the First World War. The Republic of the Slovenes, Croats and Serbs did not gain international recognition, although it fulfilled 'all the requirements laid down by international law for the emergence and existence of a state' in the view of the popular government seated in Ljubljana. This government claimed 'all state powers' and exercised them 'throughout the territory of the state' with the exception of the Prekmurje district.

The Slovene dream, and the programme for a united Slovenia drawn up in the Nineteenth Century, was finally on the verge of coming true.

But it would have remained an unrequited ambition, however, had sacrifices not been made. General Rudolf Maistre's soldiers set an outstanding example: fighting under the Slovene banner, they chased pro-German troops out of southern Carinthia and Styria. Without these territories, the new South Slav state's border would have lain further south, near Celje, and most probably Prekmurje would not have been won from the former Hungarian Kingdom at the 1919 Peace Conference. Subsequent Yugoslav histories gloss over Maistre's campaign, just as they omit reference to the fact that the Republic of the Slovenes, Croat and Serbs had been founded in the north-west more than a month before the Kingdom of Serbs, Croats and Slovenes was proclaimed in Belgrade on 1 December 1918.

Who knows how far Italy would have stretched when it came to collect the dues it had in fact been seeking since the Campo Formio Peace of 1797 and the first Italian national programme to unite 'all Italian lands' drawn up in Bassano. Although the burgeoning Italian national idea shared the same adversary as the Slovene, namely the Germans, both parties and especially the more dynamic Italians were too self-preoccupied with their future national borders to seek alliances. From the fall of the Venetian Republic (1797) right up to the battle of Kobarid and the Piave in the First World War, the aspirations of the Risorgimento steadily pushed the Slovenes back against Austria. In the fire of their unification the Italians did not even notice the Slovenes, whose renaissance was still culturally undefined.

No communication was established between them for decades, even right up to the First World War when Italy was promised part of present-day Slovenia and Dalmatia in the London Pact of 1915 in return for its crossing over to the Entente. When the Italian army started marching eastwards towards Ljubljana, after the capitulation of Austria and Germany, the Slovenes made a stand even though they had no army of their own. To challenge them they engaged a Serbian officer called Švabić and prisoners-of-war returning home from Austrian camps. Bearing the Slovene colours (a mirror image of the Serbian ones, incidentally), and in the name of the 'allied Serbian army', this improvised force repelled the invaders. Italy quickly apologised officially for its patrols which, it explained, had 'mistakenly' strayed towards Ljubljana. Serbia went on to claim it had liberated Slovenia.

The Slovenes made it quite plain that they wanted to get out of Austria. They prudently calculated that if they remained within a defeated Habsburg monarchy they and the Croatians could become a war trophy for the Serbian army that was advancing swiftly behind the retreating Austro-Hungarian army and, 'liberating' Croatian and Slovene lands without firing a shot. For years the Serbian government and businessmen had had their sights set on a Greater Serbia, and in this they had the blessings of the Entente powers which saw a strong Serbia as a bulwark against Austrian and German expansion to the east.

Soon the Slovenes had to wage the struggle for their rights and sovereignty all over again. The romantic dreams of a fraternal community of Southern Slav nations which had gradually gained sway after the Spring of Nations in 1848 shattered against the realities of the despotism that prevailed in the Kingdom of the Serbs, Croats and Slovenes.

OUT OF THE FRYING PAN AND INTO THE FIRE. Prenatal complications and an abrupt delivery produced a new Kingdom with frailties and a proneness to illnesses. From its moment of birth, the Kingdom of the Serbs, Croats and Slovenes was shaken by an unending tug-of-war between two conflicting concepts of governmental order: a federalist and a unitarian-centralist

Ptuj, copperplate engraving by A. Trost, from the book 'Topographia ducatus Stiriae' by G. M. Fischer (1628-1696)

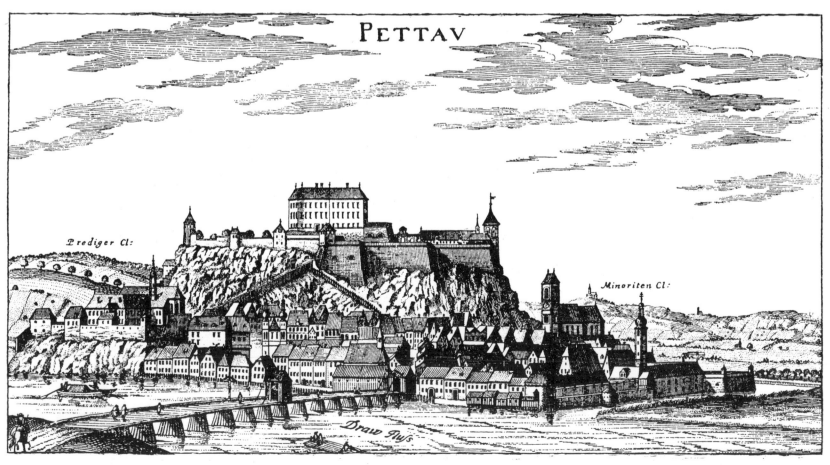

one that was championed by the proponents of a Greater Serbia and the Serbian Orthodox Church, ranged alongside the Serbian throne.

The Kingdom of Serbs, Croats and Slovenes was proclaimed in Belgrade by the Serbian regent, later King Alexander Karadjordjević. A delegation of the National Council of Slovenes, Croats and Serbs, representing Southern Slavs from the former Austro-Hungarian Empire, apparently forgot the instructions they had received in Ljubljana and Zagreb. These explicitly required that 'The final decision regarding the organisation of the new state, as a monarchy or a republic, shall be taken solely by a general constituent assembly by means of a two-thirds majority vote, no later than six months after the signing of the peace treaty. At this time decisions shall also be taken regarding the flag, the seat of the government and other bodies'.

Their 'forgetfulness' was aided by some of the Serb delegates from Croatia, 'liberals' from Slovenia, as well as pressures from the Entente allies. It also helped that some anti-monarchy Council members could not obtain passports in Switzerland in time for that critical Belgrade meeting. In short, the meeting was probably carefully stacked with a pro-monarchy majority. Fierce protests came the very day after the proclamation. Barricades were thrown up and trams overturned in the streets of Zagreb where, just a month before, crowds had euphorically celebrated the proclamation of the Republican State of Slovenes, Croats and Serbs.

Thus began the tortured, twenty-three-year journey to the demise of the first common Southern Slav state. In just a few short years, the very names were erased of the nations that had tried to found a state of equal nations. "In the interests of the unified state" they were replaced by the generic name 'Yugoslavia'. This took place in 1929 after several Croat leaders had been shot in the Belgrade Parliament and King Alexander imposed a royal dictatorship and banned the use of all national songs and symbols. Fifty years earlier even die-hard German chauvinists could not have countenanced something of the sort in the 'dungeon of nations' as Austria-Hungary was disparagingly called by its critics. The Serbian Orthodox Church became a privileged religion. The Slovenes and Croats were denied formal legal and constitutional guarantees of their equal rights, even certain rights they had previously taken for granted in 'step-motherly' Austria-Hungary.

On the eve of the Second World War, France and Great Britain began to intervene, to remedy the extremely strained internal situation and to establish contacts with the Slovenes and Croats. They sought to protect their 'legitimate interests' and forestall any inroads their rivals, Germany and Italy, might make. In 1939, Britain and France applied strong pressures on the government in Belgrade to sign the Cvetković-Maček Agreement and form a coalition government made up of both Serbian and Croatian leaders on the very eve of the Second World War.

A Croatian Province (Hrvatska Banovina) with a Croat ethnic majority was created, heralding the federalisation of the unitary monarchy. The Slovenes did not grasp the opportunity to create a Slovenian Province at that time. There was bitter opposition to the Cvetković-Maček Agreement within Serbian ranks. The radically chauvinist Serbian Cultural Club campaigned, along with the Serbian Orthodox Church, against it and Prince Paul who had become Regent after the assassination of King Alexander in Marseilles in 1934, and had husbanded the agreement through. The Serbian lobby was strongly averse to the idea of a larger, more autonomous and Catholic Croatia the Hrvatska Banovina, which moreover encompassed some Serb enclaves (precisely those that rose up in armed rebellion in the early 1990s).

WITH DILIGENCE AND TENACITY, however, the Slovenes gradually cultivated the cultural-economic autonomy of their land, the Drava Province (Dravska Banovina), which was another of the country's ten administrative units. Despite the Byzantine arbitrariness and the shaky Roman law further south, the province managed to develop faster and independently because of the strongly-rooted tradition of social orderliness, private property and enterprise. The spread of education and the foundation of the University in 1919 and subsequently the Slovenian Academy of Arts and Sciences provided strong impetus. Slovene intellectuals who had generally stayed abroad after their studies in Vienna or elsewhere began to look homewards and found more career opportunities in the new country. For Carinthian Slovenes, of course, the old capital was still closer. But the new capital was no competition for Ljubljana, which soon became a thorn in the side of the new 'unitarist' masters in Belgrade. The foundations of a national Slovene establishment and nation state were being laid.

Progress beyond these initial steps towards formal sovereignty and independence was abruptly terminated by the army's 1941 putsch against the Cvetković-Maček government for signing the Tripartite Pact with the Axis powers. This putsch, which was also understood as an annulment of the agreement with the Croats, may perhaps have 'saved Yugoslavia's soul', as Winston Churchill declared, but it plunged the country into war with the Axis powers and simultaneously split it internally, as Ustashi separatists, backed by Germany and Italy, rushed to proclaim the quisling Independent State of Croatia. The Slovenes carefully stayed on the sidelines throughout all this. Although their land was quickly overrun and dismembered by German, Italian and Hungarian armies intent on erasing Slovenia from the map, the people met the attack more nationally compact and psychologically better prepared to resist than ever before.

BARELY TWO WEEKS AFTER THE APRIL 1941 INVASION by the Axis Powers, the Slovenes formed their own Anti-imperialist' Front that quickly grew into the 'Liberation Front' and built their own 'Liberation Army'. From 1943 on, representatives of three Allied armies were attached to this army's General Staff.

At the same time, Slovene officials and delegates joined a new, embryonic federal Yugoslav parliament and government that began to be formed after 1942. The organisation of this entire movement was brought wholly under the control of the Yugoslav Communist Party which led the armed resistance against the occupying forces whilst brutally preventing any other 'liberation initiative' outside its control.

The Royal Government in Belgrade fled the country a few days after the Axis Powers attacked. The remnants of its army took to the woods to await the arrival of the Allies. It qualified the whole resistance movement led by Josip Broz-Tito as 'the work of adroit Comintern agents, well versed in manipulating noble patriots'. Be that as it may, these patriots so swelled the ranks of Tito's army that in 1943 Great Britain and the USA pragmatically began supplying and supporting it on an increasing scale as a force to be reckoned with.

The Soviet Union, which was always keen to keep several irons in the fire, was far more practical than the western Allies when the apple began to ripen. In the autumn of 1944, whilst an Allied landing was awaited anxiously, the Red Army marched across into Yugoslavia from Romania. With bearish subtlety, they requested advance permission from Tito to enter and to stay as long as operations may require. With Soviet assistance, Tito's Partisan Army proceeded to cleanse Belgrade of Nazi forces and the quisling Serbian government and, gradually established communist rule over a Serbia that was still dreaming of a unitary monarchy. The western Allies could only avert their gaze when Tito's army started settling old scores with its domestic opponents who in their 'anti-communism' had forged alliances and collaborated with the German occupying forces.

Home Guards (Domobranci) in Slovenia had always claimed they had a 'secret' anti-communist, pro-Western card they would play against the German occupying forces, which had actually armed them. But when the decisive moment to attack them actually arrived in May 1945 the card stayed up their sleeve. Instead, while the Germans were still on its soil, they proclaimed Slovenia to be a federal state of the Kingdom of Yugoslavia, notified the victorious powers and the United Nations, and 'forgot' to fire even a parting-shot at the retreating German army.

Some ten thousand Home Guards, and thousands of others from Croatia and other parts of Yugoslavia, that had fought against Tito's Partisan army, hurried to surrender to British forces in Carinthia (Austria) when Germany capitulated. Alas, the British simply handed them over to Tito's army. Very few escaped the fatal frenzy of the victorious: most were summarily shot by the Partisans. The 'inside' excuse given for this massacre was that it was essential in order to pre-empt a potential danger; merely imprisoning these soldiers for collaboration with the occupying forces would have meant they would eventually be freed by the Western Powers and probably co-opted in the impending wars against Communism. Of course it is disputable whether any such war was ever planned, but many people at the time believed the justification. But it was certainly quite deliberate, just like the Katyn Forest massacre in Poland, which was planned and blessed by the Communist International. For decades this crime effectively dissuaded all organised resistance to communism in Yugoslavia. In its wake many anti-Titoists scattered around the globe, or with the 'help' of the secret police, underwent conversion into faithful followers of the regime.

Kamen Castle near Begunje, copperplate engraving from 'The Glory of the Duchy of Carniola' by J. W. Valvasor (1689)

24. Like a national altar, Mt Triglav (overleaf) dominates the Julian Alps, one third of which lie in Italy. On the Slovenian side there are 165 peaks of over 2,000 metres. The name, dating from Roman times, probably comes from the settlement of Forum Iulii (Cividale).

25. The Triglav National Park, in addition to large numbers of chamois, now has a growing ibex population. Belief that their horns and dried heart muscles, when ground into powder, could be used to produce an elixir of youth was in part responsible for their near extermination. (pp. 36-37)

26. All the climber's efforts are rewarded by the view from the top. (pp. 38-39)

A PROCRUSTEAN BED WAS BUILT AT THE YALTA Peace Conference and it remained tight and painful for the next forty-five years. The Western Powers and the Soviet Union never deviated from the Yalta formula which divided Yugoslavia into equal 50:50 spheres of influence. To uphold it repeated purges were carried out throughout the post-war years to keep the respective 'interests' in balance. Moreover, the strains between domestic centrifugal and centripetal forces that had become so entrenched in the first despotic Yugoslavia now had to be played out on this rigid, narrow bed.

An army of highly paid 'aparatchiks' emerged and developed awesome ingenuity in conjuring up dangerous enemies, both internal and external, and inventing a never-ending succession of plausible political and ideological explanations for 'historical turning-points' and 'historical epochs' in communist Yugoslavia. One of the more attractive inventions was certainly 'self-management socialism', a unique social political order which was marketed extremely well.

In 1948, the Soviet-led communist bloc expelled maverick Tito from its ranks and imposed an economic blockade against Yugoslavia. The Yugoslav regime stood up to 'Soviet hegemony' resolutely. It gradually established credibility abroad, particularly amongst European socialists, for its 'unique road to socialism' by adopting more palatable policies at home, although some would describe them as simply more perfidious forms of coercion. Disappointed by Soviet repression in the Eastern bloc states, for Euro-socialists the 'Yugoslav experiment' was a way out of Communism's blind alley.

A new faith in a more harmonious, humane society which integrates rather than alienates the individual, gathered considerable momentum, even inside the country, as rock music and a spattering of 'grass' was allowed to seep in. It especially won a following amongst people who considered themselves to be 'Yugoslavs' rather than specifically Serbs, Croats or Slovenes. Many of these came from ethnically mixed marriages and had grown up in the relative ease and comfort of the new urban centres with their modern amenities. The standard of living was high for a socialist country despite the low general productivity, a privileged military-party-police caste and huge military expenditures. Initially, the West, helped with financing it all and later, as appetites failed to abate, recourse was made to foreign loans. 'Self-management socialist Yugoslavia' also garnered considerable international standing as the leader of the Non-aligned Movement, the Third World bloc which also seems to have crumbled into dust along with the Berlin Wall. Behind the shining facade, the elevated ideas and the propaganda image, however, raged a bitter struggle for power, a continuation of the perpetual battle between centralist and federalist forces, which ultimately culminated in the Yugoslav Army marching on Kosovo in the late Eighties, and subsequently on Slovenia, Croatia and Bosnia-Herzegovina.

AS ONE OF EIGHT FEDERAL UNITS IN YUGOSLAVIA, under the 1974 Federal Constitution, Slovenia battled more or less successfully through a maze of 'struggles for economic reform', 'social reform', 'constitutional reform', and so on. Each campaign naturally cost some experienced cadres and it was difficult to avoid the negative selection typical of all communist states. At the same time, a home-grown political-economic power elite entrenched itself as Slovenia steadily detached itself in the course of Yugoslavia's creeping 'confederalisation'. Slovenia began to see itself and to be treated as somewhat 'more equal', to use, the Orwellian phrase, than the other republics and provinces. Which indeed was rather flattering for the Slovenes.

27. *Four-fifths of Slovenia is covered by high and middle Alps intersected by valleys, where slightly less than half the population lives. Though not all of them are highlanders, a love of mountains seems to be endemic.*

28. Mists cover the mountains like a veil. Slovenia,
lying between the Mediterranean and central Europe,
is climatically a transitional country, prone to sudden
changes in weather.

29. Abundant rain, between 1,600 and 3,000
millimetres annually, makes Slovenia a green land with
lush pastures (overleaf), except for the limestone Karst
region, where surface water rapidly sinks underground.

32. It seems that Slovenes can never gaze enough at their mountains. Even early stone-age man found them attractive: remains of his habitation have been found on Mt Olševa (Potočka Zijalka, on the photo) in the Karavanke, in the Mokriška cave above Kamniška Bistrica, and in the Kamnik-Savinja Alps.

33. For some people, the view is the most important consideration when choosing a home. The majority of Slovenes, though, live at much lower altitudes and take to the heights only at weekends.

Slovenia was only the fifth largest of the federal units, a mere 7.9 per cent of Yugoslavia's territory, and about the same size as Israel, or New Jersey in the USA. Its share of the Yugoslav population was similar, and moreover on a downward trend: in the 1991 census it made up 8.3 per cent of the total population. Nevertheless, just prior to Yugoslavia's collapse tiny Slovenia was producing a quarter of the country's total exports and more than a third of its hard-currency exports. At the time its per capita Gross Domestic Product was several thousand US dollars above the Yugoslav average.

On a World Bank ranking of 200 economies at that time, Slovenia would have ranked twenty-seventh, between Ireland and Greece, quite some way behind. Yugoslavia as a whole ranked much lower.

This higher relative economic development fuelled shifts within the local communist monolith that had been set in train by the 1974 Yugoslav Constitution. The federal state had been loosened and political parity accorded to all eight units, namely to the six republics and two autonomous provinces.

NAIVETY, HUMBUG OR PERFIDY? From today's perspective, it is quite clear that the 1974 Federal Constitution could only have worked under genuinely democratic conditions, with a multi-party parliamentary democracy and a market economy. A one-party communist system could only reject true federalism, or any political pluralism for that matter, the way an organism rejects a transplant. Similarly unworkable was the sublime alternative communist ideological invention 'a pluralism of self-managing interests' in which all conflicts are resolved through a special process of 'self-managing negotiation'.

The new post-communist democracies in Eastern Europe have gone through a process very similar to that in the former Yugoslavia. It is characterised by a joke once told on both sides of the Berlin Wall before it came down. Q: Why shouldn't more than one party run for election in a communist country? A: Because then everybody would vote for the 'other' party, and you would still have a one-party system!

Some communist leaders apparently took this joke quite seriously and, hastily installed 'other' parties of their own in order to hang on to power. Serbia and the rump Yugoslavia, fell into this very trap.

Through nationalists in the Serbian Academy of Arts and Sciences, the Serbian Communist Party orchestrated a radical programme (bearing the innocuous title 'The Memorandum') to create a maximalist 'Greater Serbia', The Serbian Orthodox Church concurrently began to revivify heroic medieval myths and legends by sending long processions bearing sacred medieval relics to every corner of lands claimed to be Serbian. It became the cheerleader of Serbian chauvinism and a militant campaign to 'emancipate' a Serbia which had 'always won the wars but lost the peace' by moving its borders to places where they had never stood before.

THE YUGOSLAV REPUBLICS AND PROVINCES QUARRELLED BITTERLY in a rising mood of frustration with an absurdly bureaucratised communist system. Pressures intensified for substantive reform even at the price of anti-communism. Serbia's increasingly strident and aggressive stance naturally prompted the rest to take steps to ensure they would be their own masters. New alliances began to be forged. As the confrontation escalated demands grew for greater independence from the capital where, as in the earlier Kingdom of Yugoslavia with its Serbian dynasty, the more numerous ethnic Serbs dominated the party-state apparatus.

Not long after the death of President Tito in 1980, a campaign was launched in Serbia against the ethnic Albanians living in the Autonomous Province of Kosovo. It soon became a standard pattern, for subsequent events

34. Those who regard the national passion for mountaineering and hiking as over-rated can enjoy the grandeur of mountain scenery by motoring along the excellent road network.

in Yugoslavia as Serbian chauvinism and racism exploded into full bloom. The Albanians were accused of attempting genocide against the Serbian people, of terrible deeds like the rape of girls, nuns and old women, the destruction of churches and historical monuments. The regimes in the other Yugoslav republics stood aside whilst Kosovo was 'pacified' by federal tanks and special counter-insurgency forces. Next, the political autonomy was formally abolished of both the provinces in Serbia: Kosovo with its overwhelmingly Albanian majority, and Vojvodina, a multi-ethnic mosaic in which ethnic Serbs made up only a narrow majority.

Serbia also focussed its attention on Slovenia which, being small, typically penny-wise and circumspect, probably seemed an easy prey. The Serbian media assailed the Slovenes for being unreasonably protective of the purity of their language, labelling them chauvinists and separatists. They pushed 'Yugoslav cultural unification' by standardising school curricula throughout the country which allocated proportionately more time to a 'common Yugoslav core' than national subjects. The proportion of each national culture in school programmes was weighed on a fine apothecary's balance and mixed to a prescription written in Belgrade. Not surprisingly the first trials did not satisfy.

As the Kosovo campaign reached a climax the Serbs were infuriated by obdurate Sloven support for the Albanians. The Slovens were afraid they would be next in line after the Albanians' political and human rights and constitutional autonomy were quashed. A great public demonstration of support for the Kosovars' plight was held in Ljubljana. The Serbian regime immediately retaliated with a trade embargo, banning the sale of Slovenian goods and confiscating the property of Slovenian firms in Serbia, even though to all intents and purposes Yugoslavia was still a single, federal country.

HOT SERBIAN HEADS began to plan a mass march on Ljubljana under a banner of 'brotherhood and unity' on 1 December 1989, seventy-one years to the day after the Serbian crown had trumped the cause of the republicans and their dream of a State of Slovenes, Croats and Serbs. But this time the people-power routine that had worked so well in removing undesirable party and government leaders in Serbia, Kosovo and Vojvodina failed. Slovenia simply shut its borders and refused to let the would-be protesters enter.

The drive towards democracy in Slovenia became unstoppable. Democratic elections were held in 1990 first in Slovenia and soon after in Croatia, and clearly demonstrated that the people wanted a multi-party system, a market economy, an end to communist duress, and greater respect for human rights. But installing new, democratically elected governments was by no means plain sailing. As the new Slovenian Parliament was in the act of appointing its government in Ljubljana, federal jet fighters buzzed the city. Serbian strongman Slobodan Milošević did not mince words. He publicly threatened that Serbia would achieve its ends 'by force of arms, if necessary'.

No one had contemplated leaving Yugoslavia before Serbia started rocking the boat. There were signs that some slow progress was being made in the on-going political and economic crisis that had become an endemic feature of Yugoslavia. At least the party propaganda machine managed to create this impression in the controlled media. The process of decentralising the Federation had produced ever more powerful party-state apparatuses in each republic, with their own loyal police forces beside the mastodont federal army. Slovenia, for example, entered the Nineties with a full-blown tri-cameral parliament with 240 delegates, a republican president with no less than four vice-presidents, a prime minister with three deputies, and 24 ministers and state secretaries. It even had a state secretary for the army and another for foreign affairs: in effect, all the trappings of statehood. This was not bad as far as formal federalism went, as long as the West was prepared to foot the bill in one way or another and pamper Yugoslavia as the anti-communist Trojan horse.

SLOVENIA SUDDENLY HAD TO SHIFT GEARS as it travelled on its charted way, from a federal to a confederal Yugoslavia, and ultimately to becoming part of a united Europe. Slobodan Milošević proved to be totally intractable in the political deal-cutting. Soon every avenue of negotiation had been exhausted and there was no room left for any compromise. At a plebiscite at Christmas in 1990, almost 90 per cent of the people in Slovenia voted for a sovereign, independent state, which could join a Yugoslav confederation only as such. Events were set in train for a formal declaration of independence in June 1991.

There were no tears in the Yugoslav capital resembling those supposedly shed by the Austrian Emperor. Instead, the federal government dispatched tanks and jets to bring the errant Slovenes back into line. Whereas seventy years earlier President Woodrow Wilson had proclaimed the 'right to self-determination of nations', now the military intervention was tacitly approved by the US Secretary of State James Baker. Yet another of Karl Marx's dicta was refuted: that history can only repeat itself as farce. On the contrary, the first act of a tragedy was about to unfold.

The ruthless attack on Slovenia by the Yugoslav army is testimony that the Slovenes did not err when they chose independence. Only by the skin of their teeth did they escape the harsh fate that later befell Croatia and Bosnia-Herzegovina. Mortal danger approached as fast as Serbia's communist regime was able to move whilst tightly holding on to the reins of power and changing horses, and even its very name. Yet when all is said and done, perhaps the greatest merit for Slovenia's independence has to be given precisely to Slobodan Milošević and his supporters. This would have been quite a lark if bloody tragedy had not followed: a ten days war in Slovenia, destruction and the slaughter of many thousands of civilians and displacement of up to three million people in Croatia and Bosnia-Herzegovina, and finally carnage in Kosovo where, one should not forget, the whole tragic cycle had begun some twenty years earlier.

Enthronement of the Duke of Karantania, copperplate engraving from 'The Glory of the Duchy of Carniola' by J. W. Valvasor (1689).

51

OUT OF THE SEA OF TETHYS

THE BROODY HEN right in the central part of the political map of the Old Continent is the independent state of Slovenia. It nestles at the meeting-point of the eastern ranges of the Alps and the Apennine Peninsula to the west, and the Danubian basin and Balkan expanses to the east and south-east. The Republic of Slovenia took its place on the map of Europe on 15 January 1992, when it was recognised by the countries of the European Community. It became a permanent member of the United Nations Organisation on 22 May 1992.

The shape of this 'broody hen' is not defined by any God-given, natural borders following the geographical relief. Even geopolitics, which in theory plays an important role in drawing frontiers, was only partially influential in shaping the hen's back, namely the Austro-Slovenian border which runs along the Karavanke Mountains. All the other twists and turns were added down the centuries for countless other reasons. In Central Europe administrative and political boundaries and state borders were drawn over a millennia of shifting ownership and not, as in America or Africa, with a ruler.

The broody hen only appeared at all because the upper borderline gradually moved southwards. Centuries ago the northern border of contiguous ethnic Slovene lands once reached high into Austria. In the Ninth Century, they went even as far as Linz and along the Danube past Vienna, encompassing most of Gradiščan to the shores of Lake Balaton, which is in Hungary today. The present northern border was determined after the first Yugoslav state, the Kingdom of Serbs, Croats and Slovenes was created. At that time Carinthia, which is known to Slovenes as Koroška and to Slovene historians as 'the cradle of the Slovene nation', rejected 'Serb rule' in a plebiscite held in 1920.

Thus the frontier with Austria was drawn 'geopolitically' along the picturesque Karavanke massif, there to remain fixed even after the Slovene motherland's renewed call for the 'Korošci' to return to the fold after the Second World War. Still, decades after this disappointment, Slovenia was able to launch itself on the international tourist market as 'the sunny side of the Alps', a great marketing opportunity that would otherwise have been missed.

Our hen would have been headless had not Prekmurje, the north-eastern region stretching along the River Mura (hence the Slovene name for the area: Prekmurje - across the Mura), been wrestled from the Hungarians at the peace conference after the First World War. This finally integrated the Prekmurje Slovenes into the motherland, after being separated from their compatriots west of the Mura for a thousand years and more. Because their links with the rest of the Slovenes had been slender, just a river ferry connection, they had developed a distinctive dialect laced with Hungarian which then took its place alongside the fifty or so other dialects spoken in Slovenia. The Prekmurje Slovenes have always used their language with gusto and long cultivated it in written form.

The hen's comb is formed by the low Goričko hills rising to the north of Murska Sobota, the principal town of the region situated in the Panonian Plain. The country's northernmost point (latitude 46 53'N) is located there, above the village of Budinci. Three frontiers meet in this area where Austrians, Hungarians and Slovenes have mostly lived in harmony for a thousand years. The final shape of the hen's head was set at the 1919 peace conference. Lendava, a small Panonian town slightly south-east of Murska Sobota, with a pronounced Hungarian majority, was given to Yugoslavia in exchange for some ethnic Slovene villages along the river Raba in the far north-east corner of Slovene lands which have remained under Hungarian rule.

The Lendava River, and parallel with it the bigger Mura River flow past the town of Lendava, which today is the centre of the country's Hungarian minority. After tumbling in from Austria, the Mura quickly turns into a sluggish lowland river as it reaches the Panonian Plain. It joins the Lendava to form the border river marking the frontier with Croatia. The hen's beak is shaped by the steadily narrowing space between these rivers as they converge. It is here, in the uninhabited water meadows by the triple border, that Slovenia's most easterly point is located (16 36' E).

THE SUN KISSES SLOVENIA FOR THIRTEEN MINUTES from the moment the first rays touch it in the east to the point when the new day has begun for the whole country. Last to wake are the birds on the slopes of Muzec above Beli Potok, a small tributary of the Učeja River. The country's most westerly point, this lies on the Italian-Slovene border (13 23'E). This mountainous corner overlooks the Breginj valley, east of Kobarid. It forms the 'parson's nose', which the hen acquired, together with other parts of the Slovene coastal region known as Primorska, only after the Second World War. Previously, some 5,500 square kilometres of ethnically compact Slovene land west of a line from Mount Triglav to the Gulf of Kvarner, had been ceded to Italy along with Istria and Dalmatia. This reward had been promised to Italy by the Entente Powers for joining their side in 1915.

The hen's tail came with the peace treaty after the Second World War and supposedly corrected the historical injustice committed after the first one. Slovenia (or then Yugoslavia) regained some 4000 square kilometres of its truncated land. However some territory settled by ethnic Slovenes, such as the belt along the Adriatic coast between Trieste and Duino (Devin), and the swathe of land running northwards from Doberdob in the Karst, through the Alpine foothills to Naborjet in the Val Canale adjacent to the Austrian border remained in Italy.

To the south, the hen dips her tail in the Adriatic sea between Koper and Piran, nowadays the centre of the Italian minority. To round off our tour of the frontiers all that remains are the most southern parts that make up the Slovene-Croat border. This border has remained virtually unchanged since the Eleventh Century, experiencing only minor adjustments according to administrative divisions. There were no major changes either at the fall of the Austro-Hungarian Empire or the dissolution of the former-Yugoslavia. The excellent Atlas of Slovenia locates the most southerly point of the country at a bend in the River Kolpa near Damelj (45 25' N).

What exactly are the dimensions of our broody hen? The total length of the borders with the four neighbouring countries and the Adriatic seaboard is 1,207 kilometres. The coastal border is by far the shortest, a mere 47 kilometres. This may be a short coastline, but it is more than all Europe's nine land-locked countries have together! The frontier with Hungary is 102 kilometres long; with Italy 235 kilometres; with Austria 342 kilometres; and with Croatia 546 kilometres.

Slovenia's total area is 20,256 square kilometres, only 300 less than Israel. The Netherlands, Switzerland and Denmark are about twice as large, and Austria four times. Compared with 165 states listed by the World Bank some years ago, Slovenia ranks sixty-sixth in terms of territory. The most recent World Bank Atlas omits data concerning area. Apparently mere physical size of a nation is not relevant for an economy.

A SMALL PLACE WITH SURPRISING VARIETY geologists generally note. The primary reason for this variety is the instability of the earth's crust in this part of Europe. Right up until the recent geological past there has been abundant change: sometimes it was a sea, sometimes land, with a diversity of climates ranging from periods of tropical heat to intervals of glaciation lasting tens of thousands of years.

The surface has been unstable because of tectonic forces within the earth's core which are triggered at the point of contact of four great complexes, each of which has its own different 'living' tectonics. One of these complexes is the last, most easterly part of the Alps, which embraces a good part of Slovenian territory. Its peaks and massifs in both Slovenia and Austria rise to about 2,000 metres and above, but are appreciably lower than the western Alps. They gradually diminish as they reach the Panonian Plain, which technically starts east of a line between Zagreb and Vienna.

The eastern Alps adjoin the Dinar mountain range on Slovenian territory. Until recently this range was considered to be an extension of the Alps. However, the doyen of Slovene geographers, Anton Melik, maintains that this is only because 'the two systems have risen up so closely together that at first

Idrija, copperplate engraving from 'The Glory of the Duchy of Carniola' by J. W. Valvasor (1689).

sight one cannot define the boundary between them'. Although it is lower, the Dinar system still has high-mountain features, plateaux and karst surfaces. These two highland elements form a kind of rim to a third component: the great Panonian and Danubian plains that stretch eastwards to the Carpathian Mountains. The fourth element 'impinging' on the territory of Slovenia is the Adriatic Sea, which is described geologically as a major tectonic depression. The warm mass of water and other influences from the south account for the mild, Mediterranean-type climate enjoyed by the western parts of Slovenia. The convergence of these four complexes has produced the incredible variety within Slovenia, down to the smallest detail, individual micro-climates and even the floral compositions in the window-boxes.

SLOVENIA ROSE UP FROM THE SEA OF TETHYS during the most recent geological age in the earth's history: in the first part of the Cainozoic (Tertiary) Period, which began some seventy million years ago. The vast body of water known as the Sea of Tethys previously covered not only Slovenia, but a huge area that stretched from the Pyrenees and the Atlas Mountains in Africa, across what is now the Mediterranean to the Near East, Iran, and across to the Himalayas and the Indian Ocean. This 'flood' lasted throughout the Permian and Carboniferous Periods, some 225 to 360 million years ago.

The compacted sediment that collected over millions of years, initially in long, horizontal, relatively thin layers on the floor of the Sea of Tethys was raised to the surface by tectonic forces during the Eocene Period. In the geological events leading to the current composition and form of this part of the earth's crust, some of the land's 'building blocks' were spewed up from the sea even before the Eocene. The oldest rocks are found at Pohorje, Strojna and Kozjak in northern Slovenia, and some experts date them to a pre-Cambrian age. There are no fossil remains within these rocks, which are made up of metamorphosed sediment and magmatic rock with marble and volcanic sediments. If they really are pre-Cambrian and metamorphic, they are some 4,000 million years old. If they derive from the Palaeozoic, however, they would be a mere 410 to 590 million years of age.

Be that as it may, lead, zinc and copper ores are found together with other non-ferrous minerals in the metamorphic rocks on the southern flank of Pohorje and at Kozjak. Fossil remains in the southern Karavanke testify to their origins in a deep open sea during the Devonian Period, making them less than 360 million years old. The 600 metre-thick limestone crests found on a number of mountains also arose at that time. They contain fossilised coral, molluscs and sea lilies. Evidence of this is found on Pristovniški Storžič, Virnikov Grintovec and Stegovnik.

Geologists have identified the fossilised remains of various organisms from the middle of the Carboniferous Period some 290 to 360 million years ago when this area was submerged beneath a sea of varying depths. Rocks from the Permian Period (250 to 290 million years ago) are even more varied. They are found in the Karavanke, the northern part of the Julian Alps, along the Sava fault-line, in Dolenjska and Kočevje to the south, as well as in the area of Loka and the Polhov Gradec hills. The mass of different organisms deposited one on top of another millions of years ago and on top of rocks created in the Carboniferous Period, provide a veritable feast for the geologist.

Especially interesting are the colourful massive limestone crests with abundant rachiopods, of which there are more than eighty varieties including sea lilies and other rare fossils. The Dolžanova Gorge on the Tržška Bistrica River is a world-famous fossil site. Also from this period, if not earlier, are

35. If you half-close your eyes, the segmented landscape falls together into a single whole of peaks and valleys, mountains and plains, hills and gorges. Depending on the season, the land reveals itself as a broad snowy white undulation, or a sumptuous autumn pallet for the gods, or as numberless greens, the most beautiful shade of which is hard to chose. The fairly high Alpine massifs to the north and north-west create the iridescence. The snowy white Alps of 'appenine limestones' top the central European `tutti frutti' like cream.

36. Face to face with Stol, the highest peak (2236 m) in the Karavanke mountains which divide the Ljubljana basin from the Klagenfurt basin in Austria. It recalls Samo's country, which at the start of the Seventh Century extended from central Labia (river Laba) almost to the Adriatic Sea, and soon assumed the name Karantania. The origin of this name is disputed: it may be from pre-Indo-European kar meaning rock, or the Celtic carantos meaning friend, ally, favoured person. Places around the centre of the Karantanian state, near ancient Virunum and Gosposvetsko polje, and Krn castle/Karnburg itself, were given derivative names, such as Carantanum, Curtis Corontana, Carenta, Carantana. So too were a fair number of other places. All these names, such as the Carnic Alps, Karavanke, Karnten, Carinthia, Carnia today evoke a rocky, but pleasant and friendly, highland world.

finds of siliceous gravels, a number of zinc, lead, mercury and antimony veins along the Sava fold, copper ore and barite finds in the Karavanke, uranium at Žirovski Vrh, to mention but a few of the many geological discoveries. The Dolomites date from the same period and yield zinc-bearing ores. Lead is also found on Pohorje, as well as Mežica, where for many years it was mined.

MOST OF SLOVENIA WAS SUBMERGED beneath the Slovenian Trench during the ice ages of the mid-Triassic Period which began around 220 million years ago and was the most turbulent period in the geological history of Slovenia. The trench was a long, narrow, but quite deep sea channel. Of course it gained the attribute 'Slovenian' somewhat later! During the turbulence, the geological palette was enriched: dark slate, clays, gravels, tuffs, ammonite, volcanic rocks, marls and others broke out into the light of day. The famous mercury veins in Idrija and Podljubelj are related to the magmatic-volcanic activities taking place at that time.

To the north of the Slovenian Trench and the shallow sea, the Julian carbonate plate was created, forming the southern Alps or more precisely the southern Karavanke and the Julian and Kamnik-Savinja mountains. South of the basin rose the Dinaric carbonate plate, which extends north beyond the Dinar Mountains. Over the next million years, crests of slate clays, marls and limestone then accrued on both plates, and mostly metamorphosed subsequently into dolomite rocks. Geological events in later periods threw up deposits of the most varied ores, coal, gravels, semi-precious stones and the like.

Limestone rock deposits are the most common and in many respects the most interesting. Experts estimate that at least half the surface area of Slovenia is made up of limestone of different varieties. Around Mount Triglav, for example, the Triassic limestone is some 2,000 metres thick.

When the Sea of Tethys finally retreated in the middle of the Eocene Period, the Panonian basin gradually formed. During the Oligocene, the sea broke through the central part of Slovenia and quite possibly into northern Italy through the pass around Bohinj. In addition to the fossil-rich limestone, thick layers of lignite were also left behind in various parts of Slovenia. After powerful volcanic activity during the late Oligocene due to movement of the African and Adriatic plates, andesite tuffs from the accumulated ash remained in what are now Gorenjska and Štajerska (Styria). Further powerful folding and overthrusting in the Miocene Period threw up the southern limestone Alps (17 million years ago).

AS THE PANONIAN SEA WITHDREW eastwards, brackish water remained for a long time, until some five million years ago, in the Prekmurje region and to the east of the town of Brežice. The oil and natural gas deposits in Prekmurje are legacies of that time, as are the brown coal and lignite found in a number of places throughout Slovenia. One seam of lignite in the Velenje coalfields is an incredible 164 metres thick.

The most interesting legacies from the Pleistocene (late Cainozoic) Period, which started some two million years ago, are the residua of what were probably six alternating glacial and warm periods. Slovenia still has a number of glaciers that have shrunken since the Pleistocene and greatly altered the landscape by depositing vast quantities of moraine during the thaws.

The last of the glacial periods is estimated to have ended some 10,000 years ago. The Holocene ensued and no one has yet forecast when it will end.

37. It would be impossible to imagine the Slovene landscape without the 'kozolci' - the traditional hay racks. They are probably considered distinctively Slovene because of the number and variety found around the country. But they can also be seen on other alpine landscapes, all the way north to the source of the Drava River, and even in Sweden - wherever the rain can catch mowers and reapers by surprise. Toplarji, the double covered hayracks like these from Studor near Bohinj, are even more `Slovene'.

38. Mementoes of times bygone like this have
become increasingly scarce since 1880 when 80
per cent of the population worked on farms.
Poverty drove 300,000 Slovenes abroad, mainly
to the USA, and later to western Europe, Canada
and South America, before the First World War.
With industrialisation after the Second World War
the farm population had fallen below 10 per cent
by 1989. Today it makes up around 4 per cent.

39. *With the exception of Gorenjska and Notranjska, all regions of Slovenia produce wine with distinctive regional qualities and flavours. Since post-communist reform opened the door to private enterprise, the number of vines cultivated and the quantities of wine produced have risen steadily from one year to the next.*

40. In the Savinja valley in the central part of the country, the spring landscape is shrouded in millions of nets to guide the growth of the hops towards the sun. Up to 4,500 tons of this highly sought-after crop are grown on 66,000 hectares. Chronicles mention that hops were grown here as early as 1156.

41. Vineyards, hop plantations, trellised orchards, all of man's interventions in the landscape display his artistry. Each season of the year brings its own special beauties.

42. It is to be hoped that the
local authorities will feel
impelled to preserve the
crumbling but irreplaceable
survivors of old farmhouses,
such as this one at Kozjansko
in the Štajerska region.

43. Another example of the
rural architectural heritage,
this one in Primorska, which
is in dire need of preservation.

44. To ease communications with the outside, Slovene homes have always had verandas, balconies and terraces, which greatly enhance their beauty as well.

45. *An exceptional artistic sense is revealed by tiny details with a Mediterranean flavour.*

46. ... and the rational `urbanity' of Kras hamlets built with the skill of a swallow.

47, 48. *Traditional uses of wood and clay achieve a starkly simple beauty. Forms, dictated by function, have remained unchanged for countless generations.*

49. *The fragmentation of small-holdings that resulted from the formerly high birth rate forced many Slovenes to emigrate or move to towns. Those who have remained on the land, often carry on the old crafts to eke out a living.*

50, 51. *Whilst their timbers last, old mills and barns remain as testimonies of a passing way of life in the countryside.*

52. At the time of the 1989 survey, 48 per cent of Slovenia was farmland, though two thirds of this comprised hay-fields. Where these are not suitable for mechanized mowing, farmers normally go to the aid of their neighbours and take the steepest slopes 'by storm'.

53. When the Mura slows down on the Pannonian Plain after its turbulent entry into the country from Austria, it still has enough power, as in the old days, to turn the wheels of floating mills.

54. While devout hands decorate the Saviour in expectation of the Spring, the stork has done its part in maintaining the natural balance, placing the cradle for its new brood on top of an eyesore to dress it up a little.

55. *There are several types of kozolec. The most common type of hayrack have two uprights joined together by cross beams and topped by a narrow roof. The ravages of time make them cry out for help, which unfortunately often comes in concreted form.*

56. *Just as touching are the highland farmhouses which are now losing the residents that used to assiduously make up with love what they lacked in money. Weekenders are not a satisfactory substitute. Ecologically oriented development policies will have to take care of these highland treasures.*

57. In terms of its forest cover Slovenia resembles the Scandinavian countries.

58. In terms of pasture cover it is most like Ireland. Or should all that be the other way around?

59. If the picture looks unreal, go to Trenta and see it yourself: a mountain valley along the upper reaches of the Soča river which cuts deeply around the high peaks of the eastern Julian Alps: Triglav, Razor, Prisanek and Jalovec. Trenta was probably settled in the 16th Century when iron ore was struck. Trail-finders Julius Kugy and Henrik Tuma opened the area up for mountain-walkers.

60. *Thousands of jobs have to be done in the traditional way. It would be a pity, and a great deal more expensive, to try to modernise them.*

61. *In a few mechanised steps all the hay could be dried and stored in dry barns, but then there would no longer be such marvellous sculptures like these in this valley near Loški Potok. If the local budget cannot stretch far enough to preserve them, somebody will just have to write to the government, or UNESCO.*

77

62. When snow covers the pastures, the livestock are confined to their barns. Here in the Logar valley (Logarska dolina) the family cow seems to be waiting hopefully for the thaw to set in.

63. When spring finally arrives, it is time to wash and air all the clothes, put away the sheepskin jackets, and even get out your sun-glasses.

64-66. The distinctive hay-racks that have vanished from the Swiss cantons and many places in Austria are still numerous in Slovenia, particularly in the Kranjska region. Ethnographers attribute this to the culturally close-knit and conservative environment that rejects foreign influences.

67. On the seaward slopes of Brdo near
Gorica, laced with swirls of springtime
mists, the kozolec is unknown, largely
because the climate is so different. No deep
analysis is needed to explain why the people
here are different to the 'inland' Slovenes.

68. The spinning of flax and wool by the time-honoured method is now practised just to keep the old skills from dying out.

69. The rough hands and weather-beaten face speak of years of hard toil in the open air. Despite his cap advertising the national petroleum company, he was not a pump attendant - they are much more smartly dressed.

83

70. The hands catch the eye once again. Judging from the stillness of this granny, they would certainly deserve a rest, if only the corn and apples were not waiting there. Granny is obviously one of those people who always keep busy.

71-72. *No one prepared to work has gone hungry for a long time now, thanks in part to those who left to travel far and wide to find jobs. When the sun grows feeble, snow and ice mixed with hope and faith can be of help. But until the next spring comes, the barns with their ornamented, winking eyes, and overflowing with the last crop, are a safer bet.*

73. *Snow scenes like this in the Pokljuka area of Gorenjska (overleaf) are a favourite subject of Slovenia's naive artists, many of whom paint mostly during the winter lull in farm work.*

The Ljubljana and Celje basins were once covered by lakes which have left a deposit of sand and gravel as a legacy. In short, the modern landscape of Slovenia, including the Karst region, was for the most part created only during the final stage of the Quaternary Period.

THE TYPICAL CHARACTERISTICS OF THE KARST are related to the porous, soft limestone which is easily eroded by wind and water. They have long excited considerable interest. In fact, the first place where they were studied and explicated was in the area between Vipava and Trieste in the Primorska Kras (Karst). The word 'karst' itself comes from the old Austro-German name for the Slovenian karst lands. This name and certain terms for karst phenomena were borrowed from the local area and are today established in most languages.

The karst relief formed over a period of 20 million years and its typical features such as sink-holes and swallow-holes, disappearing rivers, chasms, caves, precipices, blind valleys and so on, attracted even prehistoric man as he searched for a safe abode with running water. The subterranean world has drawn the curious for centuries: there is Thirteenth Century graffiti in the Postojna Caves. By the Seventeenth Century interest was high enough for Lokva and Divača officials to begin charging an entrance fee for the caves at Vilenica. Today, there are around 7,500 catalogued caves that have been systematically explored, and a score of them have been fitted out for tourist visits. Visitors can descend to the deepest depths in the Škocjan Caves, which are 253 metres underground. An easy, winding path leads through one of the world's longest subterranean canyons which is more than two kilometres in length. For many reasons UNESCO has listed this cave as a world cultural and natural heritage. The Postojna Caves are more renowned, however, with their astonishingly beautiful stalactites and stalagmites, a subterranean wonder that may be toured on a small railway.

Finally, a word or two about Slovenia's climate. This is a busy admixture of rainfall, cloud cover, storms and wind, ice and snow, summer heat and drought, as well as breathlessly still air. In short, exactly the sort of climate to be expected at the meeting-place of the Alps, the Pannonian Plain, the Balkans and the most northerly corner of the Mediterranean. The place where a wonderful alchemy of natural ingredients has created, in the words of one patriotic poet, 'Heaven under Triglav'.

74. When spring comes, the early morning frost reddens little noses and makes the blood run faster through the veins. Who could imagine that this home was built in the midst of hard times a century ago, withstood all the troubles and follies since then, and yet stands untended.

THE REVOLVING DOOR OF EUROPE

FRINGES OF ADJACENT LARGE SYSTEMS MELDED into a separate whole might be an appropriate description of Slovenia as it exists within its internationally recognised borders today. It is like Switzerland, which is no 'accidental alloy' of disparate elements. At least that is the way it has come to be accepted after so much time.

Everything suggests that this territory has long been a world of its own. The Slovene lands have always attracted both traders and conquerors, whether to or merely through them. In spite of the dense forests and damp plains, they offer relatively easy passage. From the valley of the Rhône and Marseilles in the west to Thessalonika, the Morava and Vardar valleys in the southeast, there is no more convenient route to the heart of Europe than through the Bay of Trieste. The deepest indentation of the Mediterranean Sea into the continent of Europe occurs precisely here. The Alps lower their mighty barrier around its northern reaches, remoulding themselves in the shared valleys and basins at their point of contact with the Dinar Mountains.

'THE SOFT UNDERBELLY OF EUROPE' is how Winston Churchill described this area, seeing it as the best point for breaking into the Nazi fortress. The sea is separated from the Ljubljana basin only by the barely 600 meter high 'Postojna Gateway'. Long ago the Romans drove a road through this gateway and on towards the northwest, over the pass of Atrans, whose name has since mutated into Trojane. (Now it takes great will - power to slip through there without succumbing to the delicious doughnuts offered at the top of the pass to the itinerants of modern times). After crossing the Celje basin, the road reaches two barely perceptible thresholds near Konjice and Slovenska Bistrica. From there one can head for the second gate, Maribor, and go on to Austria, or for a third at Ptuj (Roman Poetovio). Roman legionaries first reached the Drava there several decades before the birth of Christ and gazed upon the inviting plains that stretch eastwards, unbroken to the Urals.

Historian Bogo Grafenauer notes that some explorers called this area the 'Styrian-Upper Carnolian passage'. This name became entrenched as the importance of different trails and transport routes waxed or waned, such as the route leading away from the port of Koper on the Adriatic to Lendava at the border with Hungary. This pathway has been regaining importance in the years since Slovenia's latest liberation, coupled as it was with Hungary's independence from the Soviet bloc, the emergence of new states in the east, and the severing of links through Croatia and the south-eastern parts of the former-Yugoslavia and Greece. Earlier, particularly after the Southern Railway was built in the middle of the Nineteenth Century, the Vienna-Ljubljana-Trieste route became vital. This changed after the First World War when with the Orient Express line linking Paris, Ljubljana, Belgrade and Istanbul was inaugurated. The advance of the Soviet empire during the Second World War had heralded the rising importance of the Trieste-Ljubljana-Budapest-Moscow route, which is once again beginning to boom.

The central part of Europe is the junction of many trade routes leading from southern Germany along the Drava River and across the Karavanke

Mountains; from the north through the Klagenfurt Basin; and along the eastern rim of the Alps from Vienna through the Graz Basin and Maribor; several routes run from the northeast to Ptuj and on to Trieste and Koper through the mountain range, or through the Vipava Valley to Italy.

Slovenia, then, is not so much a 'passage' as a crossroads , one big gateway. Grafenauer very aptly likens it to a revolving door to emphasise how often the traffic has changed directions down history. Both hordes and lone travellers have passed through this door in every direction, some tarrying, some settling, as historical circumstance dictated.

THE OLDEST UNDISPUTED ARCHEOLOGICAL REMAINS in Slovenia, two stone tools from a cave at Loza pri Orehku in the middle of the Postojna Gateway, are a quarter of a million years old. At Betalov Spodmol near Postojna archaeologists have discovered the charcoal remains and the scattered remnants of the feasts of Early Stone Age men. The bones of a hippopotamus about 100,000 years older than the tools were found at the same time in the greenish flysche clay of Postojna Caves. This animal probably became extinct here long ago when a lake that once covered the Pivka Basin dried up. Man's early forebears, who took shelter in the 'luxurious' karst limestone cave-dwellings, with water-views over both sea and lake, proved more adaptable and durable.

The Potočka Zijalka Cave lies some 200 metres below the 1,900 metre-high peak of Mount Olševa in the Karavanke. Excavating there from 1928 to 1935, archaeologist Dr Srečko Brodar discovered the bones of hunter-gatherers who had probably been chasing a cave bear. In sheer quantity these finds surpass all others in Europe from that time. Amongst the 133 bone pins found there is a proper needle with an eye. These finds, some 35,000 years old, are unique for the period. They are on display at the Celje Regional Museum and the Natural History Museum in Ljubljana. Brodar's Potočka Zijalka discovery has aroused intense interest in scientific circles because of the light it has thrown on late Palaeolithic (Aurignacian) man. It indicates there was a warm interlude, more than ten thousands years long, during the last ice-age. Had the Potočka Zijalka Cave been blocked by snow or ice, it would have been uninhabitable. The cave's cultural inventory is so important that a new grouping has

Turjak Castle, engraving from 'The Glory of the Duchy of Carniola' by J. W. Valvasor (1689)

been introduced in archaeology: Olševien. This is an excellent advertisement for the very first hotel 'on the sunny side of the Alps'.

Further research has shown that in the Palaeolithic the territory of Slovenia had major links with other cultures in the Pannonian lowlands and northern Italy. *Homo sapiens fossilis* seems to have mastered the entire process of pot manufacture, from digging up the clay and moulding the shape, through to firing at a high temperature to enable the pots to be used for cooking. The dishes used also tell us a great deal about prehistoric cuisine. Moreover, the designers clearly had an eye to combining functionality and beauty. The earthenware pots had handles or holes bored in them allowing them to be suspended on ropes. They were also decorated with drawings of serpents and other figures such as the imprint of a shell. Obviously, appearance was already a selling-point in caveman pot industry.

Humans were still dwelling in the Karst caves late in the Stone Age, between 10,000 and 3,000 BC, when their level of development was considerably higher. The Ice Age had long since passed and the Adriatic Sea had risen to flood the Bay of Trieste. The prehistoric dwellers moved closer to fertile land which they began to cultivate. The remains of settlements clearly show that copper, bronze and much later iron were already familiar. The first documented open-plan settlement in the northern Adriatic region was discovered at Žablje near Trieste. Objects from this period have also been found in caves around Aurisina/Nabrežina, Gabrovica, Duino/Devin and elsewhere. There are indications that shellfish, crab and seafood in general had already been added to the daily menu in these prehistoric times.

THE PILE-DWELLING CULTURE of the Ljubljana marshes was the next major landmark in man's ascent on the territory of present-day Slovenia. By today's standards its settlement by soil-tillers proceeded at a painfully slow rate through the Neolithic and early metal-working stages (4300-2700 BC). The obstacles were many: difficulties of access, the waterless nudity of the Karst, the overgrown river valleys and swampy low-lands encircled by mighty mountains that blocked the way to the north. Archaeologists divide this long period into three: the Impression Wave, when pots were decorated by impression, the Vlaško Cave, and the Danilo periods.

A relatively advanced culture, at least from the 'civilised' houses built on stilts, developed in the marshes and lakes around Ljubljana more or less concurrently with the last of these periods. This pile-dwelling society, known as the Ljubljansko-Barje Culture, flourished until about 1700 BC, at the transition to the Iron Age. The dwellings stood on platforms laid on top of piles hammered into the solid bottom. The wooden structures had reed walls plastered with clay, wattle and daub, and were mostly divided into a kitchen and sleeping quarters. In addition to single-family houses, there were stables, granaries, and other special-purpose buildings on stilts to serve their occupants or the community.

Around 1300 BC, this remarkable lakeside society came to an abrupt end. Judging by the charred remains of dwellings, coupled with signs that all the inhabitants seem to have fled or been wiped out at the same time it is more likely that it was destroyed by hostile intruders rather than by a natural disaster.

The millennium that followed until fortified dwellings began to be built is a blank that has yet to be filled. The first signs of fortified dwellings are found in settlements quite different from those of the cave and pile-house dwellers. Prehistoric man armed with new weapons and tools made of copper, bronze and iron was clearly more capable of subjugating possible enemies and exploiting the environment. It is very likely that the earlier, more primitive inhabitants were killed and their place taken by newcomers from other, still unidentified parts or civilisations that were already familiar with bronze and iron.

The rich heritage from the early Iron Age or Hallstatt Period (in this region from c.750 BC) and the late Iron Age or La Tene Period (from c. 350 BC) is preserved in the museums. Archaeologists have unearthed weapons and

Primož Trubar (1508-86), known as the father of the Slovene literary language.

*Title page of Primož Trubar's
'Catechism', 1551.*

tools, vessels and decorated ware of exceptional quality that tell much about the inhabitants and their way of life in these settlements. The museum in Novo Mesto has a rich collection of exhibits. Some of the drama of the times is revealed. For example, a fine copper helmet bears two wide gashes clearly caused by a battle-axe that must have been made from a harder, iron alloy. An altogether more pleasant aspect is revealed by the superb, intricate women's jewellery.

Ancient bronze vessels, iron tools from the La Tene Period, various ornaments and jewellery, as well as Roman coinage, that has been found throughout the country indicate that industry here dates back several millennia. At the beginning of this century potters were still working at Lahovče near Kamnik, where clay was being fired some two thousand years ago, and at Bukovica near Gorica, which in Roman times had been referred to as 'ad fornulos' (at the potter's). A similar industrial patrimony has been found in many places such as Bohinj, where ore was mined and iron cast back in pre-Roman times. Iron-working continued at Bohinj down to the end of last century, when tourism began to offer better returns.

A MILLION QUESTIONS REMAIN concerning the 'original settlers', 'immigrants' and all those who arrived later on the scene whether to settle and assimilate into the existing population or to move on again. The main bearers of the Hallstatt culture were Illyrian tribes (Histrians, Liburnians, Dalmatae, Japodes and others) living in the western Balkans and an area reaching into present-day Austria in the first millennium BC. The mysterious Veneti inhabited the western parts of present-day Slovenia.

In late pre-Roman times, Celtic peoples seem to have predominated in the region. By the Fourth Century BC, the Gauls, a Celtic people, are said to have burst through Slovenia's revolving door from the west, followed a century later by the Celtic-speaking Noricans who came down from north of the Karavanke. The Celts, bearers of the La Tene Culture, with its mastery of iron forging, presumably intermingled with the more numerous Illyrians and ultimately subjugated them thanks to their superior iron weapons and tools.

At the end of the Nineteenth Century, an important Iron Age site that had been continuously inhabited from about 800 BC was discovered at Vače, a delightful little village lying precisely at Slovenia's geometrical centre. At Vače and various fortified settlements elsewhere, iron and copper ore was smelted and worked into quite sophisticated artefacts. One ancient grave has yielded a wonderful, almost sumptuous, copper vessel now known as the Vače situla. The situla has three bands of decorative relief with scenes of military life and celebrations which are of exceptional beauty and unique value. It is now preserved in the National Museum in Ljubljana.

THE ROMANS COULD NOT BE STOPPED at Europe's revolving door: too many roads led to and away from it. The roads were trodden mainly by merchants carrying an assortment of the goods in demand in those times, particularly amber jewellery. They carried the precious amber all the way down from the Baltic to and through these parts to purvey to whomever was ready and able to spend lavishly for the heart of a beloved.

The Illyro-Celts were avid plunderers and their raids across the sea and into upper Italy were undoubtedly a great harassment for the Romans. In the year 181 BC, the Romans decided to protect their north-eastern border by building a powerful fortress at Aquilea, at the northern tip of the Adriatic Sea. They began systematically to subjugate the territory of Slovenia, where they met fierce resistance. Although they lost battle after battle, the Illyro-Celts kept up the fight and repeatedly sacked the Roman towns of Emona (today's Ljubljana), and Nauportus (Vrhnika). They even managed to advance almost to the gates of Rome itself. Ultimately, however, all was in vain and the Romans triumphed.

MORE THAN HALF A MILLENNIUM OF ROMAN RULE of much of this country began in about 44 BC when Octavian (later Emperor Augustus) routed the exhausted Japode and Laetobic tribes. The last shred of local resistance was finally crushed in about 9 BC and the whole territory was annexed to an empire that in development, social order and organisation, marked the zenith of classical civilisation.

Under Roman rule the territory was divided among several provinces: Venice and Istria embraced the coastal regions right up to the Postojna Gate and subsequently even further to the Karavanke Mountains; Dolenjska and eastern Styria passed into the Pannonian Province, which also encompassed the western half of today's Hungary; the northern region of Koroška (Carinthia) became a part of Noricum, which included the eastern Alps and all the lands to the Danube. The Romans razed numerous settlements when they subjugated the area, but many were rebuilt and have flourished to this day, such as Celea (Celje), Poetovio (Ptuj), Nauportus (Vrhnika), Emona (Ljubljana), Tergeste (Trieste) and Piranum (Piran). Everywhere the Romans improved the existing copper, iron and lead mines and opened new ones.

Roman rule was a boon: the land was criss-crossed with roads and new trade links were established; a government postal service was inaugurated; drinking water systems were built (one of the longest ran from Mt. Pohorje to Ptuj); baths and spas were built drawing on the hot springs; even the swamps were drained. Latin became the 'lingua franca' even among the native population, which gradually became Romanised, although children continued to be given local, non-Latin names. The Roman religion also spread through the land: shrines dedicated to the Persian deity Mithras, a cult particularly popular among Roman soldiers, have been found at Poetovio (Ptuj), Virnum in Norica (today Klagenfurt in Austria), Emona (Ljubljana) and Črnomelj.

CHRISTIANITY MADE SLOW INROADS INITIALLY, but by the Fourth Century it had started to catch root quickly and a head-on clash with the Pagans became inevitable. Theodosius, Emperor of the Eastern Roman Empire and a devout Christian finally went to battle on 6 September 394 AD against the Frankish commander Arbogasta who had entered from Gaul and appointed the pagan Eugenio emperor of the Western Roman Empire and so won over all the pagans. Theodosius marched to Vipava from Pannonia and was allegedly helped to victory by the notorious Vipava wind, the *burja*, which was blowing so fiercely that it 'deflected the lances, pushed back the arrows, and threw soldiers with metal shields to the ground'. This all took place alongside the 'Frigid River' (*Fluvius frigidus*) which most historians identify as the Hubelj River near Ajdovščina, although some argue in favour of the Vipava River. No one seems to have wondered just what went wrong with the weather.

Theodosius became ruler of both parts of the empire. But the Roman state had begun to fall apart. One testimony of the times was written down by a 'learned Dalmatian' who was beatified as Saint Hieronymus (St.Jerome). He perceived a threat to Roman culture lurking behind the increasingly frequent incursions across the Empire's borders. Hieronymus' fears and laments are recounted by the historian Gruden: 'Horror creeps over me. For twenty and more years, the blood of Romans has been flowing between Constantinople and the Julian Alps. Scythia, Thrace, Macedonia, the Dardanes, Dacia, Thessalonika, Epirus, Dalmatia and even great Pannonia are being laid to waste, devastated and seized by diverse Goths, Alans, Huns and others. Countless nobles, young virgins consecrated to God, high-minded and spiritual people have fallen prey to these wild beasts....The Roman state is being demolished....'

One and a half millenia later similar laments arose from this area. Hundreds of thousands dead, indescribable humiliation of the survivors, millions forced from their homes. Altars and holy places desecrated. Only different names and explanations were given for everything that was taking place.

The centuries of chaos that followed the demise of the Roman Empire makes it questionable whether 'perpetual' dangers and inalterable barbaric lust for other people's possessions will always lurk behind Europe's 'revolving door'. The heritage bequeathed by the Romans to these parts, and the whole of the world, is a monument to man's ascents and his falls, repeated time after time.

THE ENVIABLE WEALTH AND PROSPERITY of the Roman Empire produced more and more enemies. Avaricious attacks increased in frequency and severity. Led by Attila, the 'Scourge of God', the Huns plundered and slaughtered everything in their path. They forced their way through today's Slovenia, razing the flourishing Roman towns, even Emona. The principal target, however, was Aquilea. They could not overpower it at once and the lengthy, drawn-out assault only multiplied the suffering of the surrounding areas.

By the Sixth Century the Roman Empire lay in ruins, finished off by the Germanic tribes. Amongst them were the Langobards who proceeded to stay in part of present-day Slovenia for a short time judging from graves found at Kranj. Most of the Germanic tribes moved on northwest or into Italy, where they settled and eventually became Romanised.

Only those Romans living away from the main paths of the barbarians as they poured westwards or in compact enclaves along the Adriatic shores survived the invasions. Amidst the human torrent, now referred to as migrations, that swept inexorably westwards were the Slavs who put down roots and became the forebears of the modern Slovenes. It is estimated that the Slav settlement initially numbered about 200,000 inhabitants scattered over an area of about 70,000 square kilometres.

Devotees might think that they decided to settle because they wanted so much to spend at least their last days in this 'heaven under Triglav'. But more sceptical souls would allow that perhaps they just did not make it further west or north, bloody battles notwithstanding. Nor was there any great reason for returning to their ancestral homeland either, which moreover would have meant more rivers of blood. In time this stalemate has come to be designated the 'national' destiny.

Socerb Castle on the Italian border, overlooking the Bay of Trieste.

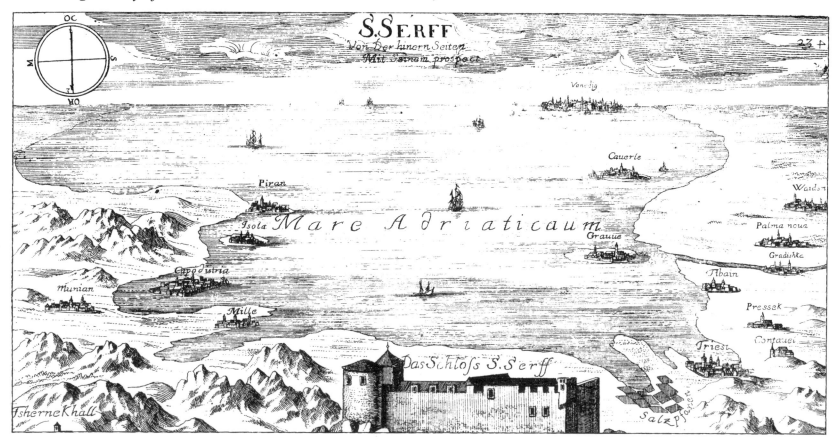

THE MIRACLE UNDER TRIGLAV

HOW THE SLOVENES HAVE REMAINED SLOVENE is certainly something of a miracle. It is a rather relative question too, for some people did not remain Slovenes and became 'strangers' instead. Namely, the Slovenes consider one of their own who has adopted another language to have renounced his or her national identity and become a 'stranger'. Language, in other words, is the very thing that qualifies one as a member of the Slovene nation. Over the centuries an indeterminate but significant number of immigrants have adopted this country and the language as their home, while others emigrated and exchanged their Slovene language for some other. All in all, given the size of the country and its dynamic history, today there is a remarkable number in the homeland and in the diaspora around the world, whose tongue qualifies them as Slovenes.

WHENCE, WHEN AND HOW the forebears of the Slovenes came to these parts is not precisely known. Most of the information about the early Slavs, some of whom became the Slovenes' ancestors, is to be found in Latin sources recording battles and other encounters with barbarians known as Sclavi, Sclaveni and similar. It has been suggested that metonymy (the association of words) came into play in the extension by the Romans of the name sclavi (captives, slaves), first to Slavs who fell into slavery and ultimately to all Slavic tribes in general. A linguistic memento of all this is the name of a stretch of waterfront in Venice where captive Slavs used to be brought to be sold into slavery: Riva degli Schiavoni.

In connection with the origins of the Slovenes, it is interesting that the ancient name *Wends* was used by the Germans to describe all Slavs. It is variously argued to derive either from the German word *wenden* (to turn hay or soil) or *weiden* (to graze or lead to pasture), or from the *Venets*, whom the Germanic tribes first encountered on the territory of northern Italy and western Slovenia when they expanded eastward. Until recently, this name was used for the Porabian Slovenes of the Raab valley in south-east Austria. Austrian Germans still use the casual form *windisch*, sometimes as a pejorative term, to describe Carinthian Slovenes.

In the second wave of mass migrations in the mid-Sixth Century which swept westwards along a wide front stretching from northern Europe to Asia Minor, the principal ancestors of the Slovenes and other Slavs crossed through Moravia to arrive at the Danube and the regions of Upper and Lower Austria. Some of them gradually settled along the Mura and its tributaries in the eastern Alps, and further south in the territory of present-day Slovenia. These migrating tribes most probably had no long-term strategic plan or any particular destination in mind. The historian Anton Melik considers that they settled primarily in places where they found cultivated fields, meadows and pastures, and not in forested areas that had to be cleared to create arable or grazing land. The continuity of the settlements established was undoubtedly linked to the continuity of land cultivation.

The precursors of the Slovenes probably settled along the Savinja and

76. *Almost every other church, or 409 churches altogether are dedicated to Mary, the Mother of God. More than a tenth of the churches and chapels are considered special holy sites and are visited by pilgrims, who are called 'romarji', a word that probably derives from Rome. The church on Šmarna gora, near Ljubljana, is a pilgrims' shrine. It is first mentioned in the records in 1435 when it served as a fortress and sanctuary during Turkish raids. The steep slopes of the hill have made it popular too nowadays as a trim trail and excursion point for people concerned more with their bodies than their souls.*

77. The heavenly scene that unfolds at this spot invites repose and meditation. So with time, many reasons for gratitude have accumulated. There is even a roof to provide shelter from the weather.

78. *The shrine built above the River Soča near Kobarid commemorates the 1.2 million people who lost their lives in this region in the First World War, between 1915 and 1917. The famous battle of Caporetto (the Italian name for Kobarid) was described by Ernest Hemingway in his novel 'A Farewell to Arms'.*

79. *Typical of the fortified churches on hills is this one at Zaklanec (Gorenjska).*

80. An aerial view of Gradišče, formerly called Sveta Trojica (Holy Trinity), with its imposing church and three belfries, in Prekmurje, bordering on Hungary.

81. The church at Ihan near Domžale, not far from Ljubljana.

82. *A tranquil scene in the upper Soča valley near Bovec. Its peace was broken in the First World War when the Italian front was established along the Soča. After it was penetrated at Bovec and Tolmin in October 1917, the front line shifted west along the River Piave.*

83. *Architect Jože Plečnik, who made a notable contribution to Ljubljana and to Prague's Hracany Castle, is justly famous for the originality of his creations. One of them is this church dedicated to St Michael in Ljubljana's Barje suburb.*

84. St Mark's church at Vrba, below Mt Stol, the birthplace of Slovenia's greatest poet, France Prešeren.

85. The unusual rotunda church at Selo near Murska Sobota in Prekmurje dates from the Fourteenth Century. Subsequently much altered, it has now been restored to its original form.

86. The baroque church by architect Matija Persky at Gornji Grad was raised in the Eighteenth Century on the site of a Twelfth-Century chapel. This was demolished on the orders of Bishop Attems to make way for the fine new church containing tombs and memorials of worthy men.

87. The surroundings inspired the builders of this church dedicated to St. George in a special way. They started to build it at Piran on the coast, around 1600. The belfry reaches high into the heavens, like the mountains on the horizon, so that departing sailors can see their patron saint for as long as possible as they depart, and as soon as possible on their return home.

88. The little two-storey Romanesque church in Kamnik has stood for many centuries. The shrine is first mentioned in 1202, but it was badly damaged by an earthquake in 1511. The lower chapel is from the Twelfth Century, and the upper from the Thirteenth Century. It is not known who did the static computations for the design, or whether anybody did, in view of the damage it suffered.

90. A church's external appearance tells of the parishioners' devotion to God or the local patron saint, and more than that. The battle for visitors started long ago, with God's help of course.

89. For man, nature has always been an inspiration for communing with the supernatural: the first wooden Christian church was built on Bled island in 800-900 AD and a pagan temple may have stood there before that, although there are doubts on this point. This Church is the fifth one built on the same spot, archaeologists say. Worshippers, and even passers-by, can make a wish by ringing a special bell inside the church. Some hotels are considering competing with bells of their own.

91. The beauties of Bohinj Lake - as the story of Bogomila and Črtomir suggests - was well known even to pagan spirits. The oldest part of St James, standing right by the lake itself, dates back to the 13th Century. The church has been renovated several times. Its frescoes from the Fifteenth and gold altars from the Seventeenth Century are renowned - adding to the attractions of these ecologically pristine surroundings.

92. Valvasor mentions that Slovenes were already making pilgrimages to the Holy Lands in 1057, and later were escorted by their elders, reputable and devout men, to Rome, Köln am Rhein, Aachen, and elsewhere. The Mother of God has always been a special object of devotion since the Eighth Century. Sveta gora (Holy Mountain) above Gorica, which has been photographed masterfully by Rafko Podobnik, is of more recent date, but nonetheless a particularly popular pilgrimage for believers from both sides of the Slovene-Italian border.

93. During the Turkish raids from the late Fourteenth to the Seventeenth century, the rural population sought refuge in churches and the fortified areas around them.

upper Sava valleys by AD 580. Soon thereafter they settled along the upper Drava and Gail rivers but they were very quickly expelled by the Germanic Bavarians that had preceded them there. Just two years later however they retook this land, with a little help from the Avars, a Mongol people who briefly ruled much of Europe between the Don and Elbe rivers in the latter half of the Sixth Century. In 598, the Slav tribes were apparently allied with the Avars in an attack on Byzantine-controlled Istria. They had discovered the 'soft-under-belly', the path along the Vipava valley, into Italy. By 611, again together with the Avars, these proto-Slovenes are said to have conquered the whole of Istria and even broken through into Furlania (today the Italian region of Friuli).

Unlike the other migrating peoples who came and went, these Slavs put down roots and gradually became the dominant population on the territory of present-day Slovenia. Various marauding tribes, the Huns in particular, are believed to have aided them in this by previously 'cleansing' most of the area, leaving a trail of destruction in their wake and reducing to ruins towns, forts and other outposts of the Roman Empire. Some historians argue that by the time the Slavs arrived, much of the earlier inhabitants, especially the Roman-ised elements, had fled to the fortified towns along the coast, so that the land was relatively deserted. Undoubtedly some of the earlier inhabitants stayed behind, as their graves and the Illyro-Celtic roots of the names of rivers and places testify.

Though the conquerors-turned-settlers appear to have later established fairly amicable relations with the remaining inhabitants, at first the native town-folk must have awaited the Slavs' arrival with trepidation. Prosperous towns such as Celeia (Celje) and Tiburnia (in Austrian Carinthia) were not only wealthy but the seats of bishoprics as well. They were fiercely defended by their garrisons. According to the records, the Slavs razed both cities to the ground, and thus erased all traces of Christianity there for two hundred and fifty years.

'OUR FOREFATHERS WERE NOT THE SERFS we are today', hot-headed Slovenes started to chant some thirteen hundred years later. At the turn of this century, when the Slovenes were squeezed back to barely a third of the land they had seized at the time of the mass migrations, they began to search historical records for heroic examples of how their ancestors had asserted their rights against oppressors. One that they unearthed recounted a Slovene elder's reply to an Avar delegation collecting taxes: 'Who of all those basked by the sun is strong enough to defeat us? We Slovenes are used to taking land from others, not having ours taken! Whilesoever there is sun, while-soever there are swords, a Slovene shall not submit!'

'Tell this to our people' writer and theologian Dr Janez Evangelist Krek urged Slovene writers. A central political figure in the last quarter-century of Habsburg rule, Krek's organisational genius contributed crucially to bringing Slovenia closer to European standards by modernising its social structure. By drawing on lessons from the distant past such as these, Krek helped weave the kind of ancient history that every nation has to have, as the priest, Franc Saleški Finžgar, wrote in the early years of this century.

Inspired by Homer presumably, Finžgar wrote the epic drama *Pod svobodnim soncem* (Under a Free Sun) imbued with the patriotism that sustained Slovenes early this century when they lived in an almost perpetually hostile environment. This book helped prepare the young generations for all their historic deeds in the two wars that followed. Finžgar's choice of setting for his tale was dictated by the historical records that were available, which were largely of Roman or Greek-Byzantine origin. But he also chose to place it in the Byzantine Empire for another reason as well. Namely, because the Slavs

94. Mt Krn, soaring to a height of 2,244 metres on the Slovene-Italian border, dwarfs the church at Drežnica, whose spire echoes its heavenward thrust.

generally had had much more success in fighting the Eastern Roman Empire and other forces in the Balkan peninsula. Moreover, these foes were more interesting and exotic, based as they were on some sort of oriental archetypes. In short they were different to the foes met on the ruins of the Western Roman Empire, such as the German tribes, or the precursors of the Hungarians.

One patriotic romantic poet, Matija Prelesnik, had earlier tried to write a trilogy drawing on the history of the Baltic Slavs, supposedly ancient Slovenes. His bitter tales of graveyards, defeats, dissension and clashes were apparently not encouraging enough even for him. He died before beginning his third tome.

Over the centuries, as the Slovenes' northern ethnic boundary drifted southwards, other Southern Slav peoples settled the expanses of the Balkans in a wide tract between the Adriatic, the Aegean and the Black Sea. Finžgar took ancient historical disputes amongst the Slavs as his subject matter for more reasons than merely colour. In an era of change and uncertainty in the Austro-Hungarian Empire at the turn of this century, he wanted to give future generations a cautionary reminder against discord within the family.

Tending the vineyard, Jost Ammon, woodcut (1567). All woodcuts are from the same source.

THE NOTIONS ABOUT THE ORIGINS of the Slovene people nurtured by Finžgar and his tales of bellicose and lordly Slavs who moved up from the southern Balkans have been shown to be erroneous. Of course, ancient Slavs did also come up along the Danube and Sava rivers, but the most likely place of origin of the majority of Slavs who settled in Slovenia is somewhere in present-day Poland. They came along the flanks of the Warta river and across the Carpathians or possibly Transylvania, through Bohemia and Moravia, thence 'directly' across the eastern flank of the Alps and into the upper reaches of the Soča valley.

Historical record (the Cividale Evangelistary from the Fifth or Sixth Century) shows that the Italians and Slovenes met quite early. According to the *Enciklopedija Slovenije* in time the western Slovene ethnic border settled between the Bay of Trieste and the Carinthian Alps, along a system of fortifications (limes) built by the Langobards to block movement out of the mountain valleys, through the Alpine foothills and Kras to the east, and the Fruili plain in the west. Until the Twentieth Century the Rossimian River near Čedad (Cividale) formed a clear divide between the Friuli and Slovene languages. From 1588, as a part of Friuli, Venetian Slovenia was officially called Schiavonia.

Not long after they had settled, a firm alliance of Slav tribes living on the territory of the southeastern Alps emerged. This alliance, forged around a compact core, was annealed by battles against Germanic Bavarians and Langobard tribes, as well as the Avars. The territory was then known as the Marca Vinedorum, 'the land of the Slovenes', and ruled by a duke with the aid of wealthy elders.

During the early decades of the Seventh Century, the Slovenes forged a military alliance with the Avars, which lasted until 626. Then the Slovene Duke Valuk joined a Slav tribal confederation across the Danube, in present-day Bohemia and Moravia, which had just been founded by King Samo (ruled 523-658), described by some as a 'Frankish merchant', and by others as a Jew with 'an exceptional talent for organisation'. Samo's kingdom extended from the middle reaches of the Elbe almost to the Adriatic Sea and was known as Karantania. The confederation, which some historians believe had its seat at the site of the present-day Viennese townships Döbling and Währing, fell apart after Samo's death. A reduced Karantania went its own separate way, continuing to exist more or less independently for some hundred years. It waxed and waned in size but the mountain-girded basins and valleys of the upper Drava and Mura rivers always formed its core.

CHRISTIANITY BROUGHT THE FATEFUL BREAK. Military fortune was fickle in those distant times. The Karantanians were sometimes on the offensive, sometimes on the defensive, engaged in interminable struggles with old rivals. Some of these enemies were remnants of the prehistoric population, while others were more recent arrivals. They included the remaining Romans, the Avars, passing Germanic tribes and other barbarians on plundering raids. The Karantanians struck various alliances as seemed expedient at the time, and broke them when fortunes changed or it suited them. These were the times of the irruption and rampaging of organised barbarian hordes that historians have labelled the Dark Ages.

A new epoch began around 740. The Karantanians joined with the Bavarians to go to battle with the Avars and Franks. They won against the Avars, but the Franks proved stronger. Under Frankish rule, Karantania remained unchanged in area until the eleventh century and for the first and only time the Slovenes lived together on equal terms under one roof.

With their innovative feudal system which operated in tandem with the hierarchy of the Catholic Church, the Franks established a new, better-organised social order which placed the Slav communities under increasingly firm control and soon confronted them with the fatal dilemma: Christianity or death. The Avars would seem to have made the wrong choice: the phrase 'disappeared like an Avar' is used in Slovene to describe someone who disappears without a trace.

Pressing olives.

'BAPTISM BY THE SAVICA', a historical saga or 'a tale in verse', by Slovenia's greatest poet, France Prešern (1800-1849), recalls the time 'when blood flowed by the town of Kranj, and dead Karantanians filled the lake' after the final battle in which the Christianised Slavs, together with their Germanic allies, overcame their pagan Slav brothers. Only the young heathen warlord Črtomir survived, all of his soldiers having fought to the death in a vain attempt to break out of encirclement. In despair, Črtomir thought of taking his own life, but his suicidal thoughts were outweighed by his yearning for his bride Bogomila, herself a follower of the 'old faith of fathers' and Živa, the pagan goddess of love. Prešern portrayed Živa's temple 'on an idyllic, safe and holy island in the midst of Lake Bled'. (Excavations under and around the present baroque church on this island have indeed confirmed that a pagan temple stood there until the first Christian Church was built over it in the Ninth Century.) However, fearing for Črtomir's life, Bogomila converts and becomes a Christian, vowing to dedicate herself to God and renounce earthly happiness in order that Črtomir might live.

When the defeated and desperate Črtomir returns, Bogomila takes it as God's mercy and persuades him to renounce the joys and pleasures of this world in favour of happiness in the next life. His initial refusal softens and he yields in the end. Črtomir is baptised at the Savica, a wonderful waterfall which spouts from the living rock above the crystal-clear waters of Lake Bohinj. Instead of conjugal life, the lovers begin an overture to celestial bliss: Bogomila in chaste longing, Črtomir as a priest of the new faith, working as a missionary among his Slovene compatriots 'far across the border'.

This tale of unhappy love projects the fate of the nation. The dramatic historical conflicts surrounding the Christianisation of the Slav tribes are personified by the dilemmas of the two young people who sacrifice their freedom and earthly happiness for the sake of their faith. "They could see nothing else in this world." But did they thereby earn their 'ticket to Europe'?

Prešern was a romantic and free-thinking spirit inspired by the French Revolution. But as a clerk articled to a provincial lawyer he subsisted in a grey, constrained life shrouded by Metternich's Absolutism. He attempted suicide twice. The destiny of this sensitive patriot highlights the angst of a member of a small nation flailing around the ankles of giants. One of his outstanding works, which include some poems in German, is *Zdravljica* (A Toast), a ballad for drinking companions. The theme of this poem was very topical for a brief but significant moment during the 1848 Revolution, and contains a first-rate political programme:

> God's blessing on all nations,
> Who yearn for that bright day,
> When o'er the sun's full stations,
> On earth no strife shall hold its sway,
> When kinsmen free all men shall be,
> Not foes but friends their neighbours see.

Prešern, the poet who encouraged the people under Triglav Mountain to sing loudly with wondrous, perilous faith in themselves, was unrecognised for a long time after his death, which is not uncommon for great artists. Since Slovenia's independence however his presence has almost become overpowering: his 'Toast' forms the text of the Slovene national anthem.

Pressing olives.

'BAPTISM BY THE SAVICA', a historical saga or 'a tale in verse,' by Slovenia's greatest poet, France Prešern (1800-1849), recalls the time 'when blood flowed by the town of Kranj, and dead Karantanians filled the lake' after the final battle in which the Christianised Slavs, together with their Germanic allies, overcame their pagan Slav brothers. Only the young heathen leader Crtomir survived, his soldiers having fought to the death in a vain attempt to defend their holy settlement. In despair, Crtomir thought of taking his own life, but these dark thoughts were outweighed by his yearning for his sweetheart Bogomila, a follower of the 'old faith of fathers,' and Živa, the pagan goddess of love. Prešern portrayed Živa's temple 'on an idyllic, safe and holy island in the midst of Lake Bled.' (Excavations under and around the present baroque church on this island have indeed confirmed that a pagan temple stood there until the first Christian Church was built over it in the Ninth Century.) However, fearing for Crtomir's life, Bogomila converts and becomes a Christian, vowing to dedicate herself to God and renounce earthly happiness in order that Crtomir might live.

When the warrior returns, Bogomila takes it as God's mercy and persuades him to renounce the joys and pleasures of this fervent life. His initial refusal softens and he is baptised at the Savica, a wonderful waterfall above the crystal-clear waters of Lake Bled. The lovers begin an overture to celestial bliss: Crtomir leaves as a priest of the new faith, working as a missionary to his compatriots 'far across the border.'

Otočec Castle in the middle of the River Krka, near Novo mesto.

THE DARKNESS OF THE NEW DAWN

AT THE DECISIVE ENCOUNTER with Christianity the Slovene tribes on the territory of Karantania numbered between one hundred and fifty and two hundred thousand people, it is estimated. They lived in village communities, in extended families or clans (zadruga), which had proven to be the most viable social organisation, best suited to the slash-and-burn farming practised at the time.

A number of zadrugas would combine together to form a župa, which was headed by a chosen local leader known as the župan. At first, every member of the community had equal rights and no one was allowed special privileges or to set himself above or apart from the others. Any attempt to do so would be punished. As time went by, however, individuals started to separate from the group on their own parcel of land, and the more skilful or capable became better-off. Some families became 'upwardly mobile'; special status was gained by the class of yeoman farmers who acquired greater rights than the ordinary peasants, probably in return for military obligations to their lords. One reason for the Slavs' fairly brief period of independence may have been their traditional inclination towards egalitarianism, or perhaps anarchy, so that they did not develop a strong feudal caste of their own. The areas inhabited by Slav tribes thus became free hunting-grounds for ever-bolder intruders who exploited the opportunities offered by this pre-feudal society.

The new foreign landowners needed money and private armies to defend themselves against barbarian invaders and to subdue tribes objecting to the imposition of taxes or the introduction of Christianity, the twin pillars of feudal society. The encroaching feudal lords divided up the land, keeping a part for themselves and allotting fields and pastures to the farmers in return for a prescribed amount of labour and a percentage of their crops. This kind of societal organisation was substantially aided by Christian ideological indoctrination. The Church itself became an enormously powerful feudal landowner through the steady expansion of its properties and lands.

THE END OF FREEDOM was heralded by Charlemagne (Karl), from whom the Slovenes took their word for king: kralj. It was Charlemagne who, in 791, wrote in one of his deeds: 'Every man who lives on this land and wants to keep his property is obliged to pay taxes; however, if he does not wish to pay them, he is free to move elsewhere...'

The great Frankish state, which was centralised by Charlemagne, needed a host of administrators, who were imported from Irish, British, Spanish and Italian monasteries. These also served as educators to teach aristocratic Frankish youths the 'seven sciences': the four liberal arts, arithmetic, music, geometry and astronomy, and the threefold way to eloquence through grammar, rhetoric and dialectics. Apart from great castles and churches in Roman and Byzantine style, the 'Carolinian Renaissance' brought educational advances.

Charlemagne plays a critical role in the story of how Christianity was brought to the ancestors of the Slovene people. His laws, intended to ensure the 'building of Christ's kingdom on earth', encouraged the first Slovene phonetic transcriptions of the prayers and other holy texts the imported missionaries employed to save the Slovenes from a pagan hell. At the same time, the church doctrine that 'secular law is given by God' also benefited both temporal and spiritual feudal lords. The more accessible Christian teachings became, the easier it was to accustom the flocks of new converts to being good and faithful servants of their masters, even to the point of fighting battles on their behalf, all of which would, of course, ensure their salvation and a place in heaven.

Fisherman.

ACCLIMATISATION TO A TEUTONIC EUROPE did not run smoothly. The Slavs rebelled and bled repeatedly, but eventually learnt the lessons of bitter experience and how to work and build in the feudal spirit. The Slovenes relinquished their practice of shifting agriculture and adopted three-year crop-rotation with fallow from the Franks, which greatly altered their life-style. They began sowing grain in the winter for a spring harvest, sowing a second crop in the spring, and leaving a third of the cropland to rest. This farming revolution soon replaced the wooden ploughshare with the iron plough and other tools.

The community decided upon the crop schedule and the pasturing of the cattle, assigning specific responsibilities to particular individuals. This arrangement lasted almost a thousand years, down to the Eighteenth Century, when various new farming techniques such as stable-rearing and fodder-feeding of cattle were introduced. But this collective decision-making somehow remained in their blood, for subsequently the Slovenes readily accepted the co-operatives and other social movements launched at the turn of the Twentieth Century by Janez Evangelist Krek and others. The priest and statesman Krek ranks as a major figure in recent Slovene history. It was due in great part to his efforts that the Slovenes began to catch up with the European mainstream. It is no mere coincidence that 'self-management socialism' was conceived after the Second World War precisely in Slovenia, and elaborated in practice most by Slovene communists.

COLLECTIVE ADOPTION of the new standards was the task of the missionaries and priests. It could hardly have been easy for them in that pagan-Slav environment: apart from the language barrier, they had to grapple with a whole host of good and evil spirits and deities. The polytheistic Slavs discovered gods and spirits all around them - in people, animals and plants as well as in water, rocks, clouds, and other inanimate objects. In the Sixth Century the Byzantine historian Procopius recorded that the Slavs 'believe in a god who strikes thunder and lightning and rules over all'. Today a visitor to the thermal spa of Moravci, or anywhere else in eastern Slovenia for that matter, might similarly be surprised to hear a local invoke an ancient god when lightning strikes, saying: 'Oh, listen to the voice of Perun!'

The Catholic missionaries reassigned Perun's role to the Prophet Elijah who is now identified with thunder in other parts of the country. Other saints did the work of various good pagan spirits and gods. Supernatural beings obviously could not be kept away from significant moments in life, such as birth, death and marriage, so the events were given new settings, new rites and customs. In spite of all this, the folklore lingered, though it naturally varied from place to place. For the most part it took the form of superstitions about evil spirits bearing illness, deafness and other misfortunes and how to chase them away with chants, special looks or a brisk action, such as spitting three times over one's shoulder.

A SPECIAL BONUS on entering the European circle encouraged the Slavs and other barbarians to adapt more quickly to the new circumstances. Besides the missionaries, priests and ecclesiastical bodies, the feudal lords also showed understanding for the problems of the pagan Slavs and charitably devised a special Slav tithe at a rate one-third lower than the usual one. The feudal lords recognised that the Slavs did not understand the Christian teachings in an unfamiliar tongue, and for this reason were 'poorly-motivated' to raise 'productivity', as we would say today, and so needed a long time to adapt to the new feudal social order.

Besides this crucial concession, the missionaries zealously set to translating prayers and other religious texts into the language spoken by the Slovenes. An example are the first extant writings in the old Slovene language, known as the Freising Memorials (Brižinski spomeniki), which Slovenes cite as the very beginning of their literature. These are so named because they were discovered in the Bavarian city of Freising, seat of a bishopric that owned extensive estates in Carinthia and Carniola settled by Slovenes. In spite of this praiseworthy orientation, the Church, namely the Salzburg Archdiocese and the Aquileia Patriarchate, which administered the territory of Karantania and sent missionaries there, became dissatisfied with the tempo of the 'acclimatisation' of the pagan-Slav work force . It started fostering the colonisation of Slovene lands by German-speaking peoples, which soon engendered conflicts that still smoulder in various forms to this very day.

AFTER LOSING ITS STATUS AS AN INDEPENDENT KINGDOM and then as a Slovene vassal principality, the territory became a Frankish county and eventually a German duchy. Whether they wanted it or not, the Slovene people came to share the destiny of the Frankish kingdom. Although they had no nobility of their own, they became directly and indirectly embroiled in the dynastic struggles that followed the death of Charlemagne. Around the year 820, a great deal of blood was shed in suppressing rebellions by Croat tribes, along with some Slovene, under the leadership of Ljudevit Posavski, the Duke of Southern Pannonia which formed the eastern part of former Karantania. At different times the Slovenes were also pressed into the ranks defending the Frankish kingdom against Hungarian, Bulgarian and Byzantine attacks.

The situation became really tense when Duke Rastislav, ruler of Greater Moravia (in what is now the Republic of Slovakia), tried to counter Frankish influence by forging an alliance with the Byzantine Empire. In 863 the Duke sent a request for aid which read: 'Our people are pagan no more, they have accepted the Christian faith, but we do not have teachers who would pass on the one true religion in our own language...' The Byzantines did not need to be asked twice. They immediately dispatched Methodius and Constantine, two erudite Greek brothers from Salonika who had learnt the language of their Slavs neighbours and already had experience as missionaries among the Tatar Khazars and Bulgars. It was said of Constantine, better known by his monastic name Cyril, that 'God has revealed the letters of all languages to him'. He is credited with devising the earliest Slavonic script, Glagolithic, which continued in use along the eastern Adriatic coast and islands until the late Middle Ages.

On arrival in Greater Moravia, the brothers, known as 'the Apostles' to the Slavs, started teaching and translating the Scriptures and liturgy into the Slav tongue (at that time not yet differentiated as national languages). Their success by using the local vernacular in Greater Moravia brought them into conflict with the Frankish church hierarchy. Charged with heresy they were

Boatman.

summoned to Rome. During their stay Constantine took monastic vows and the name Cyril, but died there soon after, in 869. In the same year, Methodius was consecrated as the first bishop of Moravia and returned to carry on his evangelical work, despite continuing Germanic opposition, until his death in 885. Thereupon, the Pope replaced the Slav liturgy with the Latin and all the disciples of Methodius, some two hundred monks, were driven out and scattered throughout the South Slav lands. Some made their way to the Adriatic coast; others went to Bulgaria and Macedonia. Both Cyril and Methodius were later canonised by the Church of Rome.

At that time, three Slav dukes in the eastern part of Karantania, Kocelj, Rastislav and Svetopolk, had successfully rebelled against the Franks and petitioned the Pope for the return of Methodius. Subsequently, Methodius became archbishop of Sirmium in Lower Pannonia, where many Slavs had settled. Under Kocelj the Karantanians reached their last brief zenith. He consolidated political and ecclesiastical independence and by then must have been dreaming about an independent destiny for the Slav peoples under his rule. However, the Frankish feudal lords were able to shatter that short-lived dream forever with the help of Svetopolk who betrayed and overthrew Duke Kocelj in 874. With his fall, the Slavs of Karantania lost their last, big chance for freedom. Discounting about six decades of raids by marauding Hungarians, henceforth the Slovenes came fully under Germanic 'occupation' for over a thousand years.

Under Prince Geza and then his son King Stephan I (St Stephen) the Hungarians (Magyars) converted to Christianity in the late Tenth Century. As their Slovene neighbours before them, they also assumed the non-optional extra of the feudal yoke. Both nations then were 'acclimatising' at much the same time. Loan words in the Hungarian language suggest that it must have been Slovene teachers who introduced them to aspects of Christianity and western European civilisation along with certain pagan beliefs still harboured by the Slovene Christian teachers. The Hungarians however proved very fast learners and the pupils soon surpassed their teachers. Nonetheless, God gave them equal reward: many centuries of German rule.

AFTER KARANTANIA DISAPPEARED from the political map, the territory was split up into duchies and counties that were granted as fiefs or gifted to the nobility and bishoprics by the Frankish king. In time, the lands were agglomerated into provinces (lands). Thus, in the stead of Karantanians we have Styrians, Carinthians, Carniolans and Istrians today. Yet a collective memory of lost freedom and the attending myths have lingered on. The utopian days when the old Slav rules prevailed are often evoked: the times when villagers governed themselves according to their own law, apportioned the land for sowing, pasturing and tree-felling and water rights. The righteous clung to the ancient principle that all disputes should be discussed and resolved communally, at public assembly, so adamantly it seems that they resurrected it in the system of self-management socialism centuries later. (A future generation will probably also want to experiment with it.)

The right of the Karantanians, alias the Slovenes, to choose their own leaders is also still very much alive in the nation's collective memory. Even now, most Slovenes know at least something about the enthronement ceremony of the Karantanian dukes between the Eighth and Fifteenth centuries. This impressive ceremony was probably unique in Europe: more's the pity that it ended before the advent of Eurovision.

97. Karst features and processes have long excited great interest. The typical swallowholes, sinkholes, polje, disappearing streams, and karst cave systems have all primarily been studied in this region, particularly in the area between the Vipava valley and Trieste in Primorska. The term 'karst' came from the old Austro-German name for the Slovenian karst lands, and today is the general international term for karstified landscapes. Pictured: the Ajdova girl on Prisanek.

98. *In the mysterious karst underworld there are three watersheds within the very small area between Postojna, Ilirska Bistrica and Divača.*

99. *The many wonders of this subterranean world are explained by the cave system itself, such as the karst hydrological system, for example, and the three underground watersheds that lie within a very small area between Postojna, Ilirska Bistrica and Divača where each droplet, brook, or river 'decides' whether to flow towards Trieste, Kvarner Bay, or towards the Black Sea.*

100, 101. Cerkniško polje (depression), flooded in winter, dries up in summer to leave just a few streams meandering across its broad meadows. The main one is the Stržen, part of the complex network of underground rivers of the Notranjska karst, which surfaces here at Cerkniško polje.

102. When underground waters rise in winter, the fields of Cerkniško polje become the Cerkniško jezero (lake), which can cover an area of 38 square kilometres, though it is never more than a few metres deep.

103. A swallow-hole (farleft), one of the many curious natural features that make the karst so attractive to tourists and scientists alike.

104. Cerkniško lake is known the world over largely due to Valvasor, and he was admitted to the British Royal Society precisely because of his description of this natural wonder. There was a time when every map of this territory had this periodic lake set in a special frame. Guided tours are now organised to view it from the best vantage points. Pictured: yet another of the attractions of the area: Rakov Škocjan.

105. A visit to Pivka jama (cave) is not for the faint-hearted or unfit. They had better make for the nearby Postojna Caves, where a small train will carry them into the underworld.

132

106. Paddling through subterranean waters is like acting out a boyhood fantasy inspired by a Jules Verne adventure story.

107.- 108. The eight kilometres long Križna jama cave on the Bloke plateau is especially beautiful with its celebrated sculpted stalagmite, 'Calvary', which stands like a huge pillar in one of the caverns, and its Cave Bear (Ursus spelaelus) Trench. The cave bear is described thus in one place: 'this beast was very useful to man: for food, clothing and for making tools from bones'. It seems that in two respects at least, the bear was of more use to prehistoric man than the other way around. It is worth noting that more than a hundred cave bear skeletons were discovered in one of the galleries.

109, 110. The fragile beauty of aragonite 'hedgehogs' and other strange creations of nature reward the efforts of dedicated speleologists, who are not few in number.

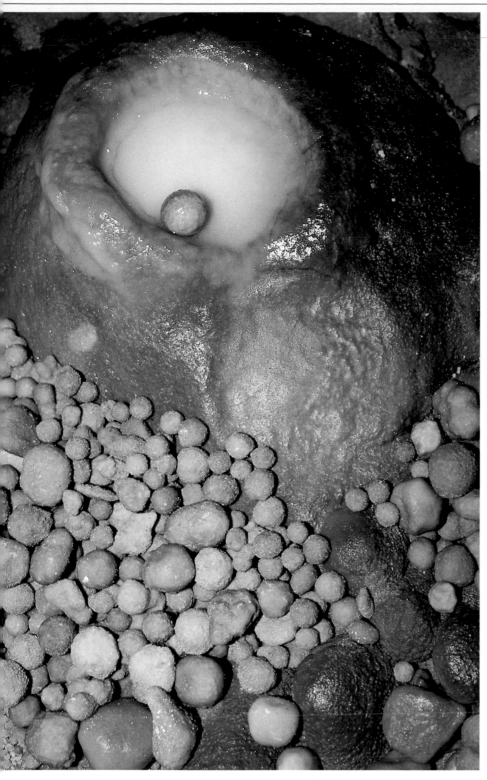

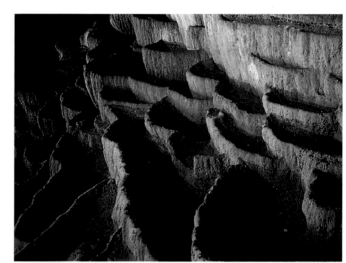

111. *A living fossil found only in the subterranean waters of the Karst is the blind* Proteus, *popularly known as the human fish because of its skin colour and texture and tiny hands.*

112. *Cave pearls is the name given to these spheres forged from stone granules in the karst foundry, the famous 'brimstone pools' in the Škocjan Caves.*

113, 114. *The infinite variety of nature's works is nowhere more evident than in the karst caves. Their wonders range from sculpted terraces to delicate 'combs' fit for a queen of the underworld.*

115. *The bones of a hippopotamus were discovered in the greenish flysche clay of the Postojna Caves. To the great sorrow of the tourist trade, the hippopotamus died out in this area long ago, probably when the lake that had covered the Pivka basin dried up. A find of some tools, traces of a hearth, and the scattered remains of a prehistoric 'banquet' for some of man's forebears, in Betalov spodmol near Postojna, dates back to the Early Stone Age, just some hundred thousand years after the demise of the hippo not far away.*

116. It is no great exaggeration to say that the Slovene's affinity for wind instruments goes back to the Olševien period. A prehistoric man appears to have used the lower jaw of a cave bear to make a pipe which can now be viewed in the Celje Regional Museum. He drilled holes in it and presumably whiled away the long winter evenings making music. There could have been some percussion too, and maybe dancing and vocals. Altogether quite some entertainment for a mountain cave.

117, 118. The petrified waterfalls, 'Gothic' columns and 'totem poles' that decorate many of the karst caves must have inspired terror and awe in the prehistoric cave-dwellers who ventured into their depths.

119. In one of the Škocjan Caves, archaeologists discovered four distinct layers of prehistoric habitation, the lowest of which contained stone arrowheads and spearheads, knives and grindstones (overleaf).

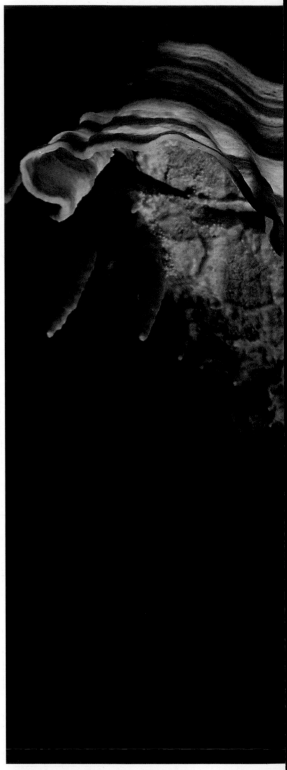

120-123. *Imaginative visitors to Slovenia's karst caves can give their own interpretation of the incredible variety of figures and rock formations. Above are the 'curtains' of Planinska jama; below, a colourful petrified 'mushroom' in Dimnica jama and the 'crystal tables' of Križna jama.*

124. Geological strata reveal that man dwelt in the Karst caves in the Late Stone Age, long after the Ice Age had passed and the surface of the Adriatic rose. Objects of copper and bronze have been found. There is also evidence that the prehistoric gastronome's menu had extended to shellfish, crab, and seafood in general. Similar objects have also been found in caves near Aurisina (Nabrežina), Gabrovica, Duino (Devin) and elsewhere. The oldest settlement found out in the open in the north Adriatic area was discovered at Žablje, near Trieste.

125. 'Enciklopedija Slovenije' mentions that Permian rocks in the Karavanke, in the northern part of the Julian Alps, in the Sava hills, in Dolenjska, Kočevska, and in the Loka and Polhov gradec hills in the vicinity are 250 to 290 million years old. They are a real treasury for geologists. The fossil-bearing limestone of Dolžan gorge near Tržiška Bistrica is especially interesting. Pictured: one new sport is descending the waterfall in Učja Valley.

126. Subterranean exploration of the karst waterways is another thrilling but risky 'sport' to be indulged in only by the fit and fearless. The water is icy and the hazards are often unknown.

127. Hydro-speeding on the Soča. This kind of racing calls for mastery of both the current and the craft, as well as fast reflexes to avoid rocks and underwater obstacles.

128. Kayaking in the impressive gorge of the Soča (left) seems safer than hydro-speeding, until one comes to the rapids!

129. Tastes differ. Some people like to lie on the hydrospeed and press on the gas; others scorn even oars and prefer to swim through all the perils. On one thing they all agree: the water is pure enough to drink.

HISTORY TURNED ON ITS HEAD is symbolically represented by the Ducal Stone (Knežji kamen), an up-ended Roman pillar taken from a nearby Roman temple. This was the centrepiece at the enthronement at Krn Castle on the plain called Gosposvetsko Polje (located seven kilometres north of the town of Klagenfurt in Southern Austria). The ceremony is described in numerous extant texts. According to a record from the Thirteenth Century, it was attended by the whole nation. The central role was played by a local peasant (*kosez*), who sat on the throne and asked the candidate duke a series of questions: who he was, would he be a fair judge, would he strive to insure the country's prosperity, would he respect and defend the true religion? During the first hundred years of the ceremony, the candidate replied personally, always in the affirmative, of course. Later, when the candidates were actually nominated by the Frankish king and did not speak Slovene, proxies answered on their behalf. The *kosez* had to be bought off the throne with gifts of farm animals, money, garments and, naturally, a tax exemption. However, he only allowed the throne to be taken after a warning slap to remind the duke to take care to be a good judge. Once he finally gained his seat on the Ducal Stone, the duke pointed his sword towards all four points of the compass.

The bishop, assisted by the prelates and monks, then held a solemn mass at the Gosposvetska church. Open air festivities would then begin. The entire ceremony was accompanied by singing and pageantry on a scale that today would require skilful stage directors, as well as large allocations from the state budget.

Lack of finance clearly was not the reason why Ernest Železni (Iron Ernest) was the last Carinthian duke invested, in 1414. The enthronement of dukes hand-picked by a foreign monarch became an empty ceremony. (Much like elections during the communist regime centuries later, when the 'list' of candidates consisted of a single name.) Further, there was widespread dissatisfaction among the peasants with the rising appetites of their feudal lords. Moreover, the Turks were coming ever closer. When Ernest Železni had been on the throne just one year, they plundered Bela Krajina and attacked the Celje region, the home of the powerful Celje counts.

Die-hard romantics still believe that the dynamic lords of Celje, who contributed the three stars to Slovenia's coat of arms, were the last chance for a native feudal ruler to arise on Slovenian soil. Alas, fate was sealed when the last of the Celje line died without an heir, a tragedy lamented to this day. The Habsburgs were more fortunate, and they steadily closed in on the Adriatic sea: Trieste and its environs were theirs by the end of 1382. Within a hundred years they had established their rule over the Goriška area and virtually the whole Slovene nation came within the borders of their realm.

THE ENTHRONEMENT OF THE KARANTANIAN DUKES is considered to be one of the cornerstones of western democracy. The ceremony endured for eight centuries, so its details naturally changed with the leader and the status of Karantania itself. However, its crux was the solemn oath to defend the country in the face of all enemies, to keep the peace, and to help widows and orphans. 'This pure democracy, unlike the Greek example and that of pre-Civil War United States, had no slaves...' writes the American author Edward Gobetz in his book *The Slovenian Heritage*. He points out it preceded by a few centuries the signing in 1215 of England's Magna Carta, that great watershed in European civilisation and democracy.

One description of the Karantanian ceremony was recorded by the renowned Fifteenth Century historian and philosopher Aeneas Silvius Piccolomini, who became Pope Pius II. He recorded in his *Cosmographia Pii*

130. Slovenia's largest cave, Postojna, is a whole underground world, a subterranean kingdom. Now that it has 19,555 meters of footpaths, its great, cavernous galleries are more like subterranean landscapes. A tour train runs through an underground ballroom, eateries and a concert hall that can seat ten thousand people.
There are around 6000 registered and professionally explored caves in Slovenia. Around twenty are open to tourists. The deepest down a visitor can go is 253 meters at the bottom of the world's longest underground canyon in the Škocjan Cave. This cave is listed by UNESCO as part of the world cultural and natural heritage. There are hundreds of deep sinkholes in the Karst region, of which three are more than a thousand meters deep.

Papae that 'there is no known symbolical democratic ceremony anywhere else in the world'. A century later, the French philosopher Jean Bodin, in his work *The Six Books of the Republic*, held that the ceremony had no match anywhere in the world. Bodin's work was studied by none other than Thomas Jefferson, author of the American Declaration of Independence, who reasserted everything that Bodin had written about the enthronement of the Karantanian dukes. Other scholars argue that the ceremony exemplified the historical basis of the theory of social contracts, whereby the ruler undertakes specific obligations to the ruled in return for the right to govern them. By relating the Karantanian experience to what was happening to the American colonists of his time, Jefferson was able to validate the legitimacy of the American struggle against the British: it was the British who had broken the contract with the people by imposing a system of 'taxation without representation' on their colonial subjects.

Although in time the ceremony on Gosposvetsko polje in Carinthia degenerated into mere show, it was imprinted on the national consciousness if only through the language. Slovenes call Carinthia the 'cradle of the nation' and the significance of its myths was heightened after the formation of Yugoslavia in 1918. It was Carinthia's 'cruel misfortune' to be 'torn from the fold' when in 1920 it opted at a plebiscite to remain in Austria rather than join a Yugoslav state under a Serbian king. Of course the Carinthians, and their children and grandchildren today, could retort that the 'cradle' has remained in the fold and it is the others who have strayed to the wrong country.

The Ducal Stone, now preserved in the Klagenfurt Museum, was pictured on the first Slovene bank note issued after independence in 1991. This provoked outrage in some Austrian circles with protests against a symbol of Carinthia, a part of Austria, being used as a symbol of a foreign state. But the issue subsided quickly amidst the generally favourable view in Austria of Slovenia's declaration of independence and the good neighbourly relations between the countries.

THE FIRST FIVE HUNDRED YEARS OF THIS MILLENNIUM largely fixed Slovenia's physiognomy down to the present day. Many of the villages and small towns that arose in this period stood on sites settled in earlier times by the Illyrians, Celts and Romans. Their growth was hastened by the influx of those fleeing from the rapacious feudal lords who vied with each other until the beginning of the Fifteenth Century. The eight crusades between 1095 and 1291 failed to bring the promised 'salvation from Muslim hands for the towns sacred to the birth and life of the Lord', but they most certainly strengthened the position of the Central European rulers and feudal aristocracy. The presence of these forces and the order they imposed enhanced the spiritual and temporal power of the lords who were in close alliance. The nobles equipped armies, founded fortified monasteries and monastic orders of knights and the like, to defend against invading hordes irrupting from the south and east. At the same time, traffic at this crossroads of nations was growing as demand for oriental goods that had been 'discovered' during the crusades grew and generated great profits.

Because the feudal lords had problems with the Slavs even after their Christianisation, they began to bring other, dutiful settlers into the region, particularly from German-speaking lands. It is often claimed that ethnic differentiation was not yet in fashion then: the newcomers merely belonged to this or that master, sometimes to the ruler of a wider region or state, but their dialects or languages were not yet crucial issues. The argument that national feelings, peoples and nations are of a later date cannot be refuted. But it is

Printer.

hard to believe that the missionaries accompanying settlers from Salzburg felt the same empathy for their 'own' members of the flock and others with different tongues. Oglej (Aquilea) was kinder than Salzburg not because of its Mediterranean climate but more likely because it did not have a 'tribe' of its own. Empty tracts of Friuli had been settled by Slavs in several places, and a compact Slav territory was established in Istria.

The feudal lords and clergy plainly counted on their 'own' people who were distinguished by their tongue. The study of tolerance could have begun a long time ago, at least after the meeting called by Charles the Great in Rižana (Istria) in 804. The Istrian townfolk complained about Duke Ivan who ruled Istria at the time, we learn from Josip Gruden's *History of the Slovene Nation*: 'He took away from us the forests where our ancestors used to gather hay and put the swine to graze. He took our tithed villages and placed Slavs on our land where they are ploughing our fields and pastures, mowing our grasslands, grazing our pastures, and paying tithes to Ivan from our land. They are taking our oxen and horses. If we complain about it, the Slavs say we should kill them ourselves. The Duke has also taken away the houses which our forebears ran according to their custom... For three years we have had to pay the tithes, that should go to the holy Church, to the Slavs which the Duke, to all his shame and our ruin, put on the lands of the Istrian churches and the Istrian people.' In reply, Duke Ivan promised to go himself to see what was really happening: 'if they can stay there without harming you, they may stay' otherwise they would be expelled 'to wastelands.' After all, did not these Slav dukes call for uprisings, reckoning precisely on their 'own' subjects?

Between the Tenth and Twelfth Centuries the newcomers cleared the forests near existing settlements and built new 'villages', 'dorfs' which in time acquired qualifiers like New, Upper, Lower, Black added to the name of the original settlement. Later the new settlers had to seek land at higher altitudes, sometimes even as much as 1,000 metres above sea level. The newcomers were settled in a fairly systematic manner, especially in the northern areas where the Slovenes soon found themselves living in islands in a German sea. By the end of the Fourteenth Century, mixed areas were only to be found in Carinthia. The dividing-line between the two ethnic groups was not as clear-cut there as it was along the German border.

THE ETHNIC CRYSTALLISATION that ensued is referred to as 'Germanisation'. Branko Božič in his *History of the Slovene Nation* records that Slovenes finally disappeared from the Tyrol, Upper Styria and a large part of Carinthia in the Fourteenth and Fifteenth Centuries. Until the Nineteenth Century, the Slovene-Austrian/German boundary ran from the town of Hermagor (Šmohor) in the Gail (Zilja) valley in the west, over the Gailtaler (Zilje) Alps, past Villach (Beljak), and across Lake Ossiacher (Osoje), thence eastward, north of the village of Maria Saal (Gospa Sveta) to the peak of Grosser Speikkogel (Golica) and on into the western foothills of Slovenske Gorice Mountains. From here it passed Bad Radkersberg (Radgona) and continued east to the German-Hungarian border, across the River Raab (Raba) to the town of Szentdotthard (Monošter).

German settlements lying within these reduced Slovene lands (36,000 square kilometres smaller) were mainly concentrated in the Val Kanale (Kanalska dolina), the Kočevje district, Selška Sora valley and around the village of Ratitovec. A 'big island' of Bavarian and Tyrolian Germans between Kranj and Škofja Loka was the first to meld. The great champion of the *Glory of the Duchy of Carniola*, Johann Weichard Valvasor, observed in the late Seventeenth Century: 'In the village of Bitnje they speak half German, half

Paper-maker.

Carniolian, and the mixture is so bad they cannot be understood even if one knows both languages perfectly...'

The medieval colonisation abated with the growth of towns and trades and crafts such as iron working: the harbingers of the industrial age. There was, anyway, less and less land available for tilling. The forests were needed to provide fuel for the smelters, and cleared land was mostly used for grazing. The pulse of the towns quickened offering new prospects, particularly for those fleeing feudal bondage.

Back-breaking toil was expected of those who worked the land, for feudalism was only little removed from slavery. Besides labouring a certain number of days a year on the feudal estate, the peasant farmers had to give their lords a percentage of their harvest. The masters eventually realised there was more to gain by giving the peasants more land to till for themselves rather than compelling them to work on their estates. This encouraged the tenant farmers to work harder and produce more, bringing higher taxes to the feudal lords. The lords steadily raised their levies, and as if that was not enough, the *župans* also started collecting taxes. The *župans* had evolved into small landowners, a kind of minor gentry, and actually became the highest class of Slovenes. Nonetheless, as a study of medieval land registers reveals, all the strings were still held by the feudal lords. They laid down the law and acted as judge, jury and castigators of any wayward peasant under their jurisdiction. As 'God's representatives on earth', they meted out severe punishments for non-fulfilment of obligations and other breaches like rowdiness or petty theft.

Ethnic crystallisation during Medieval times led to more and more confrontation between the Slovene peasants and the German nobility with their stewards and bailiffs who were mostly men of Slovene origin who had thrown in their lot with the foreign nobility and became alienated from their fellow countrymen.

THE ADVANCE OF THE TURKS AND OTHER CALAMITIES cast dark shadows over the glow of Christianity. Plague, famine and wars decimated the population and struck such terror that the prayers beseeching protection against them have survived even to this day. The Black Death, as the epidemic *Yersenia pestis* was called, ravaged Slovene lands fairly often. In his writings, Johann Weichard Valvasor records eleven epidemics between 1230 and 1649. The most devastating outbreak of this terrible disease, most commonly transmitted by fleas and rats, was in the middle of the Fourteenth Century, when it is assumed to have spread to the coastal towns of Koper and Piran from Dalmatia. In seven years, some fifty million people are estimated to have died throughout Europe and Asia. The scourge of the Plague was indelibly imprinted on the popular memory and features in works by the noted writers Ivan Pregelj, France Bevk and Vladimir Kovačič.

Apart from the earthquakes, locust plagues, severe winters and droughts which were not lacking at the time (though the rulers did not use them as excuses for a badly-run economy in those days), the Ottoman Turks soon became public enemy Number One. The first great invasion occurred in 1415, just a year after the last coronation in Gosposvetsko Polje. The Turks plundered the Celje area, the southern regions of Bela Krajina and Dolenjska, and the environs of Ljubljana, though the town managed to defend itself.

Around the time of the fall of Constantinople in 1452, Serbia lost the last vestiges of its medieval independence and was incorporated into the Ottoman Empire. Over three and a half centuries, the Turks descended upon

Slovene territory on a regular basis, sometimes several times a year. On their rampages they penetrated as far north and west as Friuli in Italy and Carinthia. In his chronicle of Austria, Carinthia and Hungary, the priest Jacob Unrest from St Martin by the Drava vividly describes the incursions: They captured the men, old and young, and killed them; abused the women and took a great many people away with them; they ransacked and burned all of the churches...

In later times, the Turkish raids were also the subject of a number of literary works. Last century, Josip Jurčič, the first real Slovene novelist, wrote a story inspired by the Scottish writer Sir Walter Scott about a young boy who was kidnapped by the Turks, trained in the army and later, as an invading janissary, recognised his old home village.

When the suffering had become unbearable and Europe was in turmoil in the face of the Turkish advance, hope appeared in the form of the Hungarian king, Matthias Corvinus. At the head of his army, he not only successfully checked the Turks, but invaded northern Bosnia, whence from he was able to penetrate deep behind the Turkish lines. Corvinus soon became renowned as a saviour and benefactor, and because he was good and fair, the Slovenes have attributed him a role never played by any Slovene.

Cerkniško, the periodic lake studied by the polymath J. W. Valvasor.

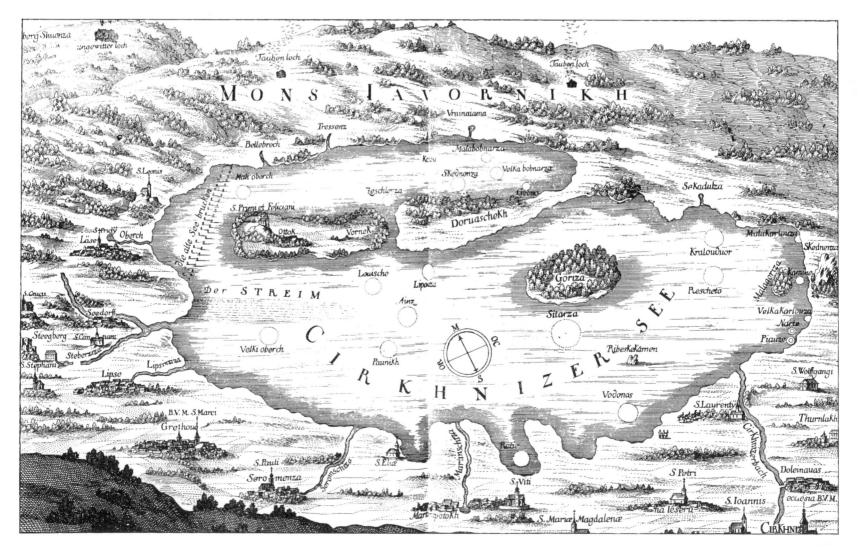

WAITING FOR KING MATJAŽ

A MONUMENT HAS YET TO BE ERECTED to the bravery and sacrifice of the Slovenes and Croatians as they served for three hundred years at the ramparts of Europe. The bloodshed began once the Turkish army had overrun the greater part of the Balkan Peninsular and struck across the Sava River for the first time, in 1391. Its light cavalry and mobile infantry outmatched the obsolete formations of the Christian knights who tried in vain to check their plundering raids. An even more serious flaw in the overall defence was the dissension, bickering and selfishness that precluded effective joint resistance.

WHERE HISTORICAL FACT ENDS and myth begins is sometimes very difficult to judge, especially when dealing with the past of a small nation. Over-shadowed by powerful nations, small ones have often been neglected by mainstream historians and chroniclers, which then leaves a lot of room for tailoring stories of the past to suit specific tastes and needs. Where authentic sources are lacking, the national fantasy can often fill the gaps with as much seeming credibility as genuine historical facts, and perhaps even more. This has been the case with the Serbs in particular over the past century. Myths became accepted facts and unquestionably affected relations amongst the peoples of the former-Yugoslavia.

The epic ballads of the largely illiterate people transmuted the dire times following the battle on the Marica River in the collective consciousness. One ballad is about Prince Marko who succeeded his father, Vukašin, as the feudal lord of Prizren. This national hero is still affectionately invoked in Slovene as well as Serbian folk songs as Kraljević Marko. Although he became a Turkish vassal and by strict modern criteria was little short of a collaborator, he is lovingly portrayed as bravely outsmarting and fooling the Turks. Although he actually lost his life fighting on the side of the Turkish forces against Duke Mirćet of Wallachia in 1395, he has been enshrined in folk memory in these regions as a faithful protector from the Turks.

National myths and folklore have likewise obscured the famous battle between the Serbs and the Turks fought on the plain of Kosovo Polje on St Vitus' Day, 28th June 1389. The defeat pitched the Serbs into five hundred years of vassalage to the Turks, or 'struggle for liberty' as it is usually described these days. For the Slovenes, Croats and Hungarians it meant being placed in the front-line of defence of the Christian world from Islam. Thereafter Serbian soil became the springboard for Turkish raids across the line. The first incursion into Slovene land, near Metlika took place in 1408, the next in 1411.

Long and convoluted arguments ensued within Christian ranks as to how best to bring the foe to his knees. The situation is only too familiar for anyone who has lived in the Twentieth Century. They devised systems of speedy communication using bonfires, arrows and the like, and procedures for bringing valuables inside fortifications, although the serfs were often left outside to fend for themselves. Complications arose when the systems had to be financed. However, Habsburgians, Celjans and others from more distant areas took part in the defence.

THE SLOVENE PEASANTS' BATTLE AGAINST FEUDALISM, like the war against the Turks, was protracted and lasted several centuries. It had begun as soon as Karantania became a Frankish territory, after the aborted revolt of Ljudevit Posavski, with whom the Slovene people had been allied. Incorporation into the Frankish Kingdom brought a number of far-reaching consequences. Slovenes could no longer establish an upper class of their own and the Frankish nobility slowly degraded the *kosez*, the Slovene landowning class, to the level of servitors who gradually lost their national identity. When a number of towns started burgeoning in the Thirteenth Century, most of their dwellers were foreign settlers from other countries, and the Slovene minority belonged to the lowest classes of the townsfolk. It was only after peasants were given permission to move to the towns, that Slovenes gradually came to form the bulk of the urban population.

The feudal lords and landowners, who exercised their authority through officials known as *valpet* and *birič,* constantly tried to raise the *stara pravda* (old rights or dues) exacted from the peasants. The main *pravda* or *cinz* was paid in grain or cheese and the *mala* (small) *pravda* in produce for the day-to-day needs of the feudal household, such as craft wares. When money gradually superseded barter in kind, the peasants had to give their feudal lord approximately one-fifth of the value of their yield in cash. A vestige of feudal ties persisted up until the end of the Second World War in Brda, in western Slovenia, where the landless *koloni* had to give half their yields to their landlords.

New ways of milking the lower orders were devised by the nobility with great ingenuity. Homesteads were virtually looted when the head of the family died. Even the local priest made sure to get his share, too. Livestock was taken from the stable as payment for funeral services, and penalties were meted out to the family if the deceased had not taken the last sacraments before death. These hardships were compounded by the miseries caused by continuous clashes amongst the feudal nobility, like the battles after 1456 for the inheritance of the Counts of Celje, and finally the Turkish incursions. The peasants rebelled frequently and the final outcome was declining harvests and rising poverty.

AN EXODUS FROM THE LAND. By the late Fifteenth Century around 15 percent of farms had been abandoned in the Ptuj area, about a third in the Karst, the Vipava valley and in the environs of Ormož and Slovenj Gradec, while as many as half stood empty in the Posavje region. The wave accelerated as the feudal lords tried to exact even higher taxes from the remaining tenants to make up the shortfall in their revenues. In an effort to hold back the tide in some places laws were passed prohibiting farmers from moving to the towns or to another feud. Nevertheless, in the Brežice area in the south of Slovenia, no less than three-quarters of all homesteads were deserted.

The exodus further intensified when more liberal state and city policies permitted migration into the towns. These new town-dwellers, the predecessors of the industrial proletariat, lived in shacks near the iron foundries and supplied wood and charcoal for the works, as well as undertaking all sorts of other jobs. A section of the nobility did their utmost to put a brake on the accelerated development of towns, the cottage and craft industries and iron works - the catalysts of the urbanisation process.

The marauding Turks also took a dreadful toll. Sometimes they stayed on Slovene soil for several months at a time and food would become scarce as everything available was requisitioned to feed the soldiers. The loss of life was huge. The county records in Upper Carniola, Styria and Carinthia indicate that by 1508 the Turks had killed or taken prisoner approximately 200,000 people from those regions alone. There was ferment amongst the peasants. Resistance was spreading. Associations began to be formed, called *Bund* in German and *Punt* or *Puntarji* in Slovene, with the aim of rolling back the rights of the feudal masters to just those laid down in the *urbar* (the feudal land and taxation register) and prescribed by the *stara pravda*. An uprising seemed imminent, and for the first time in several centuries all the Slovene-speaking people banded together wearing evergreen sprigs and cockerel feathers in their hats. But once again, they lacked a powerful leader.

This is something that they never found and always had difficulty admitting. So the collective imagination solved the problem by adopting King Matjaž, a ruler that never was.

THE GENESIS OF THE MYTH of King Matjaž, which helped generations of peasants endure the miseries of feudalism, has been illuminated by recent studies. The Slovenes' greatest folk hero, has been traced back to King Matthias Corvinus of Hungary (and Croatia), who acquired his name from the raven (Latin: *corvus*) on his coat-of-arms. Matthias was associated with present-day Slovenian lands only briefly before his sudden death, yet in blithe disregard for the facts, folk songs and tales have elevated him to the role of mythical King of the Slovenes.

In a sense Matthias Corvinus was predestined to be bound to Slovenia and its people. He was once betrothed to a lady of the Celje house. His father, Janos Hunyadi, the elected viceroy of Hungary, had attempted to form a broad regional alliance against the common enemy, the Turks. The Albanian, Skenderbeg, was the only leader to accept Hunyadi's call. The Serbian ruler Despot Branković, who was a vassal of the Turks, firmly opposed the idea even though his daughter, Katarina, was married to Count Ulrich of Celje. Hunyadi (called Janko Sibinjanin in Croatia where he is also a local folk hero) proceeded to go to war against the Turks and led his army deep into Serbian territory, as far as Kosovo and fought a three-day battle, in 1451. The Hungarians were badly defeated by the Turks and their Serbian vassals. Despot Branković managed to capture Hunyadi and held him for a huge ransom. He also extracted an agreement on the marriage of his eleven-year-old son, Matthias, to Elizabeth, daughter of Katarina and Ulrich II of Celje and granddaughter of Branković himself. This liaison with the mighty Matthias Corvinus could have changed Slovene destiny. But it did not come to pass. Elizabeth died at the tender age of fourteen, and the counts of Celje were left without heirs.

In 1453 the Christian world was shaken by the news that Constantinople had fallen to the Turks. Hunyadi again set forth with an army to drive the Turks back across the Bosphorus and out of Europe. This time he got no further than Belgrade, where he stayed to help break the Turkish siege of the city. Hunyadi died of the plague two years later, at nearby Zemun, and command was assumed by his firstborn, Laszlo who soon made his mark in Slovene history.

Laszlo bore a grudge against Ulrich II of Celje for supposedly slandering his deceased father, Janos. When Ulrich came to Belgrade to the aid of Frederick III of Habsburg in November 1456, Laszlo ambushed and killed him with a mighty blow of his sword, splitting his skull. Convincing testimony to this can be seen in the Celje Museum, where the cleft skull is on display. The scandal that ensued was so great that besides Laszlo, his brother Matthias

132. The village of Šmarje between the Vipava valley and the Karst began, like many settlements, as a few cottages and a churgh protected by earthworks or a wooden palisade. In some cases, these were superseded by one or more rings of stone ramparts.

133. The Istrian village of Kostabone, high above the River Dragonja, which marks the border here with Croatia. The mellow stone houses were clustered together for safety along the top of the ridge, while the steep slopes were used for cultivation. The walled cemetery with cypress trees is typical of this region.

163

134. Štanjel, an excellent example of a fortified medieval terrace settlement, stands on a site first inhabited in the Bronze Age, strategically located on the edge of the Karst plateau. Work is now underway to restore the semi-deserted village and its castle, originally Romanesque but later much reconstructed.

135. Žužemberk, one of several castles in the valley of the River Krka in Dolenjska It was heavily damaged in the Second World War, when it was used as a stronghold by anti-Partisan forces, but has been partly restored.

136. Monasteries played a major part in Christianisation, defence and education of the population. Eleven different orders were present in Slovenia.
The Benedictines were one of the first to arrive and became especially prominent, followed by the Cistercians with their manuscripts, and the Carthusians who now reside in only one of their four monasteries, Pleterje (pictured) which Count Henrik II of Celje founded in 1407.

137. Dobrovo Castle reigns over the gentle hilly landscape of Goriška Brda on the border with Italy. This building replaced the original castle on the site, which was probably destroyed during the Venetian-Austrian war at the beginning of the Sixteenth Century.

138. Kamen Castle near the village of Begunje in the foothills of the Alps. First mentioned in 1263, its owners included the counts of Celje and the Lambergars, one of whose members, Gaspar, won 85 tournaments and is celebrated in a folk ballad for his battle against the giant Pegam.

139. At Bogenšperk castle, above Litija, J. W. Valvazor conceived of Slovenia's greatest promotion ever, his 'Glory of the Duchy of Carniola'. He committed all he had to this huge work, and incurred heavy debts to carry it out. He had to sell his vast library and his castle. Nothing like that could happen to the author of the present book. He has no castle.

140. Brdo Castle near Kranj, probably
early fifteenth century in origin, has had
a number of famous residents, from the
enlightened Baron Zois in the Eighteenth
Century to Prince Regent Paul
Karadjordjević in the 1930s and
President Tito. Set in grounds covering
some 500 hectares, it is now a hotel and
the home of the International Centre for
Management Studies.

141. Rihemberk Castle above the village of Branik beside the Sežana-Nova Gorica road is one of the largest in Slovenia. The circular keep with walls three metres thick is thought to have been raised on Roman foundations in the Fifteenth century. Badly damaged in the Second World War, it is now undergoing restoration.

142. Above Škofja Loka, one of the most beautiful of medieval towns, is the imposing castle which, like the town itself, was rebuilt after the earthquake of 1511.

143. The baroque chateau of Štatenberg, built by Baron Dizma Attems between 1720 and 1740 in the hilly, winegrowing Haloze region in the east of Slovenia. With its interior lavishly decorated with murals, sculpture and stucco, Štatenberg is considered the most beautiful residential building in the country.

144. There are many deserted, crumbling castles around the countryside. When or whether they will revert to their owners or their heirs is unclear. If they reach the market instead, some bank or finance group will hopefully be found to catalyse renovation and adaptation that will bring life back to their halls.

145. The Baroque manor of Dornava, some 5 km from Ptuj, was built in fairly grand style around 1700, at the site of the former Dornava homestead which had burned down. When he bought it some thirty years later, with the assistance of an Italian architect, Count Dizma Attems 'created a unique totality of the manor's architecture and the landscaped park', in the words of art historian Ivan Stopar.

146. Bled Castle, perched on a cliff above the lake, is nearly a thousand years old. Now a fascinating museum, it is visited by many of the holidaymakers who flock to Bled, one of the earliest centres of tourism in Slovenia.

147. Snežnik Castle in the Notranjska region is named after the nearby mountain. A fortification existed here in the Thirteenth Century, but the present castle is mostly of later date.

Corvinus also fell into disgrace. The inherited rivalry with the Habsburgs nevertheless brought him to the throne. Matthias was elected Hungaro-Croatian king two years later.

Historians remember Matthias Corvinus as a good and skilful ruler who formed the first centralised state in central Europe and brought under control the feudal anarchy that had paralysed effective resistance to the Turks. It was he who checked the progress of the Turks, even ejecting them from parts of Bosnia, and going on to establish the provinces of Srebrenica and Jajce, which subsequently formed part of the *cordon militaire* known as *Vojna Krajina*. This spared Slovenia any more Turkish invasions for the rest of the 1460's.

THE TURKISH TERROR RETURNED WITH A VENGEANCE during the 1470s. The Ottoman forces rampaged through the Croatian districts of Lika and Istria and penetrated into present-day Italy, with the ultimate goal of seizing Venice, their appetite having been whetted by the rich Venetian cities in Dalmatia. In 1478, Venice was steeling for an attack, but at the last moment the Turkish army turned north along the River Soča and into Carinthia, where they laid waste the countryside for over a month. It has never been made clear just why the Turks changed course then. The Turks raided Slovenia several more times up to 1483, but on each occasion Corvinus' troops managed to partly protect the unfortunate population. Corvinus resisted the Turks bravely but he was not always consistent. The Venetians, namely were his rivals. It sometimes happened that his warning systems on the ridge tops, the cannon shots and the like, 'broke down' during the Turkish assaults against Venice. A lull of eight years of peace that he then negotiated with the Turks won Corvinus eternal honour among the Slovenes.

Incensed by the indifference of other European rulers and the Pope, Matthias Corvinus used this peaceful pause to settle accounts with Frederick III of Habsburg. He became embroiled in a ten-year war during which he occupied Vienna, in 1487, and held a major part of Slovene territory from 1479 to 1490. Although his troops did their share of pillaging, Corvinus did not lose favour in the Slovene folk memory mostly because the Turkish attacks ceased during his rule. However, his sympathy for peasant rights also greatly endeared him to the people.

Corvinus' court became the gathering place of prominent humanists of his day. In Bratislava he founded a university, and in Budapest a theological faculty as well as the Corvinus Library, a treasure house of ancient manuscripts and prints. This all added to his reputation which grew so rapidly that the Slovenes naturalised him as 'Kralj Matjaž', adopting him as their own monarch soon after his death in 1490.

A SPATE OF HEROIC UPRISINGS marked the opening of the Sixteenth Century. The Turkish invasions had exacerbated the plight of the peasants and in self-defence they formed a well-organised Peasant Alliance. Those who joined paid a membership fee, which was used to purchase arms. Threats and sanctions such as being prohibited from using common pastures and forests or even attending church pressured non-members to join. The rebel peasants' proposals were quite revolutionary: they wanted commoners to be appointed as local magistrates and the right to approve the appointment of priests. Equipping themselves with arms for defence against the Turks proved a very clever move since it gave the peasants a certain amount of political leverage. In places in the northeast the Alliance threatened the nobles with disobedience, crossing over to the Turkish side, and even with

148. The mighty fortifications around the little church in Hrastovlje, in Rižana Valley just north of Koper, create the impression of a castle as they shield it from assault. Hidden behind the high walls is one of the most valuable art treasures in Slovenia: a tri-nave Romanesque church from the Twelfth Century. Janez of Kaštel painted the Passion of Christ and, more importantly, the famous late Gothic 'Dance of the Dead'.

emigrating to Italy. (Nearly six centuries later, a separate 'home guard', the Slovene National Defence Force, had similarly shrewdly been formed, parallel with the regular Yugoslav army, and was later skilfully deployed to extricate Slovenia from the former-Yugoslav state).

When the first major uprisings had spread across Slovenia in 1476 and swept through practically the whole province of Carinthia, the day was saved for the feudal lord by the Turks. They came in from Friuli across the mountain pass and surprised the peasants during their preparations to march against their masters. The Turks killed and captured about a hundred. This turn of events prompted the Carinthian priest Jacob Unrest to comment: 'And God, who never deserts the righteous, came to their aid and punished the peasants' infidelity by means of the heathen Turks. So did God in order to prevent disloyal peasants from shedding Christian blood...' Nonetheless, some years later the unrest swelled into the greatest such rebellion on Slovene soil: the Peasants Revolt of 1515. The insurgents' demanded respect for the *stara pravda* (the old rights or dues), an end to all the violence and arbitrariness of certain feudal lords, and the lifting of taxes imposed by local lords.

At that time the Habsburg Emperor Maximilian was at war with the Venetian Republic over possession of the port of Koper and the inheritance of the counts of Gorica, and he was anxious to calm the unrest in his realm. He had previously banned the Peasant Alliance but now received its leaders and graciously promised to appoint special commissioners to investigate all their complaints and ensure observance of the *stara pravda*.

'THE CASTLE ON FIRE, THE COUNT HAS FLED, THE WINE IS FLOWING, LET BLOOD BE SHED...' are the words of a Slovene song recounting the events that then unfolded. Whether the Emperor meant to keep his promises, and whether the feudal lords would have accepted them, was never known for the hot-headed peasants went into action before their leaders returned from the imperial court. A blood bath ensued. The peasants attacked, captured and razed to the ground many castles across the Slovene provinces. Quite a few nobles lost their lives beneath the walls of their castles as the strains of the peasants' revolutionary march echoed throughout the land. This march, preserved down the ages, was sung in defiance against the Axis occupation forces during the Second World War. Since the occupation forces and their Slovene collaborators had turned many ancient and stately castles into their own fortresses many more of them were damaged during that war too.

Of all the peasant rebellions of the Sixteenth Century, the most inspiring was the Croatian-Slovene mass uprising of 1573. Its causes were described by Grand Duke Charles Habsburg, who wrote: 'Here...the nobility treats cattle better and with more respect than they treat their underlings. Unable to protect these poor souls from Turkish tyranny; they squeeze them dry and persecute them just as the Turks do...'

The 1573 uprising was probably the very first example of systematic co-operation in the history of these two neighbouring peoples. It was led by Ambrož Gubec, who was quickly dubbed Matija (possibly in connection with the myth of Matthias Corvinus), and his commander-in-chief Ilija Gregorić. They were both experienced si in fighting the Turks, but that was a defensive war. This proved to be a critical weakness of the rebel army's offensives which failed to achieve the ambitious goal: abolition of all taxes and levies and custom duties imposed by the temporal and spiritual lords. The rebels paid dearly for their shortcomings at battles near Krško, at Bistrica ob Sotli and Šubice along the present Slovenian-Croatian border. The feudal armies reinforced by *Uskoki* mercenaries who guarded the border against the Turks, slayed thousands of rebels before breaking them entirely.

The masters' revenge was horrible. Gregorić was decapitated. Gubec, whom the peasants had wanted to make their king, met an even worse end. He was put on a red-hot throne in the centre of Zagreb and a red-hot 'cattle-muzzle crown' was placed on his head. Then he was drawn and quartered. Villages and markets that had abetted the rebel peasants before or during the uprising had to pay huge fines. Rebels who survived the massacres were tortured and their hands, ears, noses were cut off.

Well-formed national feelings hardly underlaid the uprising. However the same or similar language obviously brought the people together and identified and named them - as Slovenes or Croats. This set them apart from the others, which was often good enough a reason for being abused by their masters.

PROTESTANTISM, AS A CURE for the cancer that for centuries had been spreading through the corpus of the Catholic Church, quickly won followers in this land. Winds of dissatisfaction and protest were already blowing across Europe in 1517 when Martin Luther posted his 95 theological theses on the door of Wittemberg Castle church in Germany.

By then it was a rather common occurrence in Germany and neighbouring countries for rebellious peasants to take up arms against their feudal lords. There were other kinds of social conflict, as well. The townsfolk wanted trade to be controlled, which did not suit either the nobility nor the farmers. Within the governing class itself there was a clash of interests too: landowners wanted a free rein in running their estates, while the rulers sought to tighten their control over the feudal lords. Relations within the Church

Lake Bled, copperplate engraving from 'The Glory of the Duchy of Carniola' by J. W. Valvasor (1689)

179

were exacerbated by the moral decay: the higher clergy, which came from the ranks of the nobility, held all the key positions and lived a life of luxury; the lower, uneducated ranks, sought to emulate their superiors by engaging in business of various kinds, savoury and unsavoury.

The humanistic ideas emanating from Italy and other west European centres doubtless contributed to the climate in the both the Church and society at large in the later Middle Ages. These ideas drew on a revival of ancient Greek philosophy giving priority to empirical knowledge, and openly questioned particular religious doctrines and dogmas. As moral decline accelerated within the established Church, and no mean number of its members obviously failed to practise what they preached, many people returned to the bible and the 'original principles' of the faith. Martin Luther was convinced that salvation could not be bought with the indulgences made available to frightened sinners after 1507 from sellers directly licensed by the Pope. He questioned papal infallibility and other dogmas. He preached that the only way to strengthen one's faith and gain God's mercy was by reading and observing the prescriptions of the Holy Bible. This had only recently become feasible with the invention of the printing press by Johannes Gutenberg in Mainz in 1445. Literacy was spreading and Protestant teachings were being disseminated through Luther's translation of the New Testament into German, and other translations of the Bible into the vernacular.

THE PATH TO A PROTESTANT SALVATION was opened up for Slovenes by Primož Trubar (1508 - 1586). Just how far they were prepared to follow it is another story, of course. Trubar's life led him from Rašica near Velike Lašče, in the southern region of Dolenjska, into the folds of the Reformation spirit, particularly in Trieste, where he studied at the school of the bishop and poet P. Bonomo. The *Enciklopedija Slovenije* relates that he became acquainted there with M. Ceroni and G. Terenziani, studied Italian, Virgil, Erazmus of Rotterdam and his famous *In Praise of Folly* , J. Calvin and Italian renaissance literature. Though Protestantism failed to become entrenched in Slovenia at that time, Trubar remained loyal to the ideas of the Reformation throughout his life despite persecution and expulsion. He fled to Germany, but his attachment to his homeland fired his desire to bring to the Slovene people 'the doctrines of true Christian religion, knowledge essential for the welfare of the soul and the greatest comfort to every man'.

Trubar produced the first two Slovene books, *Katekizem* (Catechism) and *Abecednik* (Primer) in Tübingen, Germany in 1551. He signed the latter with a pseudonym 'a patriot from Illyria' and dedicated his work to 'the poor, simple, good-hearted Slovene people... so that their language may be both written and read, like the languages of other nations...' He wrote his first two books in the Gothic script and the next twenty-four in the Latin script.

Among Trubar's confreres were Jurij Dalmatin who translated the Holy Bible (1584) into Slovene, and Adam Bohorič who wrote the first Slovene grammar book. All three spent most of their lives in exile abroad, apparently drawing inspiration from the very persecution designed to thwart them. Together these three virtually created the written Slovene language, basing it on the Dolenjska dialect as the standard. Trubar must also be credited with starting up primary education, and it is also thanks to him that Ljubljana got its first high school. As a priest living abroad, he paid special attention to the education of gifted Slovenes at German universities. At his urging efforts were made to spread the Protestant faith among the Italian and Slav peoples. He organised the printing of reformation literature in the Glagolithic and Cyrillic alphabets. Altogether he was a skilful Protestant public relations

Merchant.

manager. Particularly intriguing was his utopian idea that Europe should pacify the Turks by converting them to Christianity.

Trubar's fiercest opponents were, of course, at home. When supporters of the Roman church prevailed in Slovenia, in contrast to most of Germany, Switzerland, Scandinavia, Britain and parts of France, one of the main tasks of Counter-Reformation commissions everywhere was to search out and burn Protestant books which were being sent in in great quantities. Soon however, the Bishop of Ljubljana, Tomaž Hren, a conscientious Counter-Reformationist, successfully petitioned the Pope for permission for Catholic priests to use these books, because they could not replace them quickly enough.

In short, to carry the day, the Counter-Reformationists had to concede some of the demands of the reformers: to tighten discipline, raise moral vigilance within the church, restore standing in science, cultural and public life. The Jesuits had a special mission to assist the restoration of the Catholic Church's authority in the Protestant countries by pursuing what was in many respects the very program of the Reformation! Bishop Hren had bowed to the right of the common people to listen to sermons and read the Bible in their own Slovene language. Once again, the invention of the printing press fostered literacy, and was of immense importance in the development of the Slovene national identity. For a nation that had not been quite sure about its own name, the written language became a catalyst of national consciousness.

Pedlar.

BEFORE THE TELEVISION ERA, the only way to escape oppression was through ingenuity. Of course, in those days not everything was doom and gloom. After the death of Matthias Corvinus, when the Turks again started to attack the territory of present-day Slovenia, the emergent national feeling, evidenced by the growing use of terms such as 'Slovenes', 'the Slovene language', 'Slavs' and others, was strengthened by the occasional victories achieved on the battlefield by local commanders such as the Auerspergs, the Counts of Turjak, particularly Herbard who governed the province of Carniola and was commander-in-chief of the Military Frontier (Vojna Krajina), and Weichard who commanded the Karlovac fortress and the whole Krajina region. But it was Andreas of Turjak who won the most glory in one of the Christians' greatest victories over the Ottomans, the battle at Sisak.

On 22 June 1593, Andreas led his 300 armoured men, draped with tiger skins, into battle against Hasan Pasha's army near the town of Sisak in Croatia. The Pasha had spent three years preparing to raze the mighty Karlovac fortress that had been impeding his raids into Slovene lands and territories further to the north and west. As far away as Ljubljana people were frightened and getting ready to flee. However, the Turks were crushed by the combined Christian forces so badly that they were unable to mount another such assault again.

Thereafter the Bishop of Ljubljana celebrated mass on that date wearing vestments made from Hasan Pasha's cloak. But this did not quite satisfy the folk imagination which wanted a hero. Unlike the Hungarians and the Croats, who had a true king, hero and Renaissance man in the figure of Matthias Corvinus, the Slovenes had to invent their monarch, King Matjaž, from scratch.

In the folklore, various historical figures began to meld together to create a Slovene king who was a composite of Matthias Corvinus, Kraljević Marko, Janos Hunyadi, Matija (Ambrož) Gubec, Ulrich II of Celje, as well as some Homeric heroes from ancient times. The many versions of the life story of this invented king were garnished with various exotic episodes: in one he was imprisoned in a Turkish dungeon and was set free at the request of the

Sultan's very own daughter; he ran off with a Turkish beauty, whilst his wife waited for him at home for ten long years and was just about to re-marry when he popped up amongst the wedding guests, and other fanciful tales.

Nearly all the stories and adventures of King Matjaž have the same unhappy end: after losing a battle he is retreating with his army when a mountainside opens up revealing an underground cavern which they enter. The King and his army fall asleep at a round table made of stone and ivory which encircles a linden tree. But King Matjaž still has work to do: he will awake when his beard has grown long enough to circle the table three, five, or sometimes nine times, or on another version of the legend, when a brave young man draws Matjaž's sword from its scabbard. Many people have already entered the cavern and tried, but the soldiers would begin to stir, and they had to run away in terror.

What will actually awaken King Matjaž will be a cry for help from his people: when all the hardships, injustices, taxes become insufferable; when new recruits are needed for the army, when the true faith falters... King Matjaž will come to their aid. The meeting place will be under the great linden tree, which will burst into leaf, and then King Matjaž will lead his troops to victory over all enemies, kings, all emperors, if necessary the whole world. The old faith and justice will prevail and a glorious age will be ushered in for the Carniolans and Slovenes.

All that is needed is to wait and, of course, not turn on our television sets.

Postojna, cooperplate engraving from 'The Glory of the Duchy of Carniola' by J. W. Valvasor (1689).

MATJAŽ IS NOT COMING

THE COMMON DESTINY OF THE SLOVENE PEOPLE had probably been a matter of concern to their neighbours even before the Slovenes, scattered throughout various feudal lands, realised themselves that it might be wise to discuss their future together. Historians rightly note that nation states as we know them today did not exist in Europe until at least the Seventeenth Century. Nevertheless, by the turn of the Sixteenth Century, the process of Germanisation had taken away a great chunk of territory once held by the ancestors of the Slovene people. It had been done in a planned, methodical fashion (rather similar in essence to the recent ethnic cleansing in the Balkans).

The growing awareness of common roots was very likely encouraged by the first book written for 'dear Slovenes' by Primož Trubar and his Carniolan students at the University of Tubingen in Germany. It would have been greater, had the Protestants heard and supported the peasants' social and other demands instead of insisting on their duty to obey God and the 'just' feudal lord. Humility and the constant repetition of prayers and psalms in their own language was prescribed as a sure way to find reward in heaven. However many of the common-folk seem to have wanted an advance payment whilst still on earth. By the end of the Eighteenth Century the peasants had rebelled against their foreign feudal lords some hundred and twenty times. On a dozen occasions or more they attacked various high-living and immoral clergy and monks who were prone more to *dolce vita* than a spiritual life.

The peasants' only victories were against the Turkish invaders, which did not bind the lower classes together or give them a sense of nationhood, probably because they were not in their own national army and had no nobility or ruling class of their own. After the battle of Sisak in 1593 the Turks did not return again to Slovene lands other than the southern frontier towns of Metlika and Črnomelj, and in 1683 the Prekmurje region on their way to break down the gates of Vienna. Finally, the Turks withdrew from Central Europe under the peace treaty signed at Sremski Karlovci (now in Serbia) in 1699.

A new epoch began to unfold. Economic and social change started to bring down the borders separating Slovene lands, encouraging greater mobility and strengthening the bonds between the descendants of Karantania. At times it seemed somebody was drawing King Matjaž's sword from its scabbard and that the saviour was awakening.

THE DAWN OF THE NEW AGE for the Slovenes came by accident two years before Christopher Columbus landed on the shores of the Americas. One fine morning in 1490, an unknown cooper was trying to lift a new barrel which had been left overnight to soak in the river somewhere near the confluence of the Idrijca and Nikova rivers, not far from present-day Idrija. From beneath an imposing pile of rocks he spied something even more brilliant than the crystal-clear waters. The cooper took it to a gold-smith in nearby Škofja Loka, who identified it straight away as quicksilver, the metal mercury. By 1494, this rich deposit was being mined commercially.

149. This fearsome dragon, the emblem of Ljubljana, crouches menacingly on one of the bridges over the Ljubljanica, the river that flows through Slovenia's capital.

The first capitalist iron-making also dates from this period. Iron production and the expansion of foundries reached their first peak by the Sixteenth Century when water power was harnessed to fill the bellows and lift the heavy hammers. These pioneering large mining, smelting and foundry enterprises were mostly financed by merchants who provided credit for new tools and equipment, as well as victuals for the poor.

The initial years were lean for Idrija, but the mine soon started to reap solid returns on investment. Within thirty years 50 tons of mercury and cinnabar was being produced annually. Between 1539 and 1573, output rose to some 1,650 tons of mercury and 300 tons of cinnabar, which was sold on the European market and even overseas. However, the owners' luck ran out at the end of the Sixteenth Century, when the mine was 'nationalised' and taken under state control in order to 'make better use' of it. Since in time, two-thirds of the profits ended up straight in the pocket of the Habsburg emperor, he clearly had no desire to yield Idrija to anyone, except to Napoleon when he was so compelled.

In contrast to the small initial mines that farmers worked by primitive methods to supplement their income, Idrija's deposits and booming demand on a huge market, soon turned it into an altogether different sort of operation. More and more efficient methods of mining and organisation and a variety of spin-off manufacturing and processing technologies were developed. With returns of two to four hundred per cent on invested capital at the mine, the small town of Idrija grew into 'one of the biggest sources of European merchant capital'.

THE FOUNDATIONS AND BUILDING BLOCKS for future industrialisation were all in place: there were abundant mineral resources, plenty of water to provide energy, and international trade routes. The most important centres of iron-working were Javornik and Jesenice for iron and steel, then Bohinj, Kamna Gorica, Kropa and Tržič - all in the Gorenjska region; Železniki on the river Sora, noted particularly for the production of nails and horseshoes; the Goriške ironworks in the upper reaches of the River Soča, Mislinja in Styria, and Zagradec in the Dolenjska region. By the end of the Seventeenth Century, metal production in the province of Carniola (today's Gorenjska and Dolenjska) and the Gorica district was estimated to amount to some 1,650 tons per year.

In the course of the Sixteenth Century, a variety of manufacturing plants were opened throughout the land. One, the Vevče mill at Fužine near Ljubljana, was the forerunner of one of the most modern paper mills in Slovenia. It was one of the first to be bought up by foreign investors following the end of the socialist era. Cannonballs were cast in Ljubljana and the cannons themselves made in Celje. In Ferlach (Borovlje) rifles were made, and still are. Glass-works were prospering all over, particularly in the capital Ljubljana and at Radgona.

Crafts seemed to be flourishing everywhere: in the Gorenjska region they were spinning flax and weaving linen, in the Gorica district they manufactured silk, and in Dolenjska and Notranjska, where cool conditions and bitter winds prevail, wool was spun and woven. At Stražišče and Bitnje near Kranj they produced such large volumes of material for sieves that it was sold across Europe, even as far as Spain and England. Wood-working, practised throughout the country, was especially concentrated in the southern areas around Kočevje and Ribnica, in the Loška dolina region and in the vicinity of Postojna. These areas exported a wide variety of small wooden articles, in as many as a thousand shipments a year, all over Europe.

150. The oldest relics of Ljubljana, the jewel of the Ljubljanica River, are urns from the Early Iron Age. The earliest inhabitants of this former marshland were the pile-dwellers from 3000-1700 BC. The Romans later built Emona, and were later replaced by Slavic tribes. This history is all coded in the genes of this composed city and, although it is not present to the eye, many are smitten by it. This view shows the Church of Mary of the Annunciation, from the middle Seventeenth Century, whose marvellous Baroque façade defines the very heart of the city.

151. *The Fountain of the Three Carniolan Rivers by Francesco Robba was raised in 1751 in front of Ljubljana's Town Hall (Rotovž), which dates from 1485. The building was later renovated in the baroque style and altered again after suffering earthquake damage in 1895.*

152. *Panorama of Ljubljana from its ancient castle on a hill which rises in the centre of the city.*

153. Ljubljana's fabric and urban planning owe much to Jože Plečnik, Slovenia's most distinguished architect, who wanted to embellish the Ljubljanica with as many bridges as possible. This one is the Cobblers' Bridge (Cevljarski most), so named because of the shoemaker's shops in the vicinity.

154. One of the rare monuments of gratitude to Napoleon outside France is to be found in Ljubljana. It is inscribed with an appropriate ode by Valentin Vodnik.

155. Plečnik's most famous bridge (in fact, three joined together) is Tromostovje. The department store topped by a statue behind it is one of several notable buildings in Ljubljana in the Secession style.

*156. In summer, old Ljubljana beside
the river is a favourite place for outdoor
eating or just chatting with friends over
a glass of beer or wine. Both beverages
are produced and drunk in large
quantities in Slovenia.*

*157. Following the reconstruction
programme for the old part of Ljubljana,
these venerable buildings along the
Ljubljanica mostly conceal modernized
interiors.*

193

194

158, 159. In the first half of the Eighteenth Century, Ljubljana acquired a number of fine baroque churches, such as the Ursuline church dedicated to the Holy Trinity (opposite), with altars carved by Francesco Robba, and the Cathedral (above). Giulio Quaglio painted the interior of the Cathedral, which was modelled on the Il Gesù church in Rome.

160. The severe lines of Ljubljana's
modern architecture contrast with a more
ornate building by Secessionist architect
Maks Fabiani from the beginning of the
century.

161. Many are not enthusiastic about the
buildings of Ljubljana's business centre,
but at least they scarcely impinge upon the
medieval and baroque architecture of the
older part of the city.

162. A bird's eye view of Ljubljana with Tromostovje (centre) in front of the church of Mary of the Annunciation, the cathedral (top left), Robba's fountain and the Town Hall (top centre).

163. In some towns like Celje ancient monasteries have gradually become completely incorporated into the urban fabric. This Minorite monastery was founded by the Counts of Celje before 1242. The counts remained its principal patrons and chose the church as their last resting place on earth.

164. Maribor, Slovenia's second largest city and the centre of Štajerska (Slovene Styria), is mentioned as a centre of trade in the Thirteenth Century, when it was known by its German name of Marburg. It was later fortified with walls, strengthened in the Sixteenth Century, when it was besieged by Sultan Suleiman II

165. Maribor's sixteenth-century Town Hall with its clock tower (top) is one of many buildings of architectural interest that have been preserved in the old part.

166. Metlika in the Bela Krajina region bordering on Croatia bore the brunt of many Turkish attacks between 1408 and 1578, especially before the construction of Karlovac fortress.

167-168. The greenness of the two quite different and distant towns shown side-by-side here is not the only thing they have in common. Both are border towns. Old Slovenj Gradec (left) stands near the border with Austria, while recent Nova Gorica (right) has mushroomed on the plain, left of the second bridge and the railway line, lying along the border with Italy. The `old' Gorica (Gorizia) went to Italy under the peace treaty. Both towns are well-aware of the importance of building bridges and ties with neighbours and the world at large. Slovenj Gradec boasts of its UN and UNESCO sponsored art gallery. A spirit of internationalism is steadily melding the two Gorica's.

169. Ptuj on the Drava, one of the oldest and most attractive towns, stands on the site of Poetovio, the largest Roman city on the territory of present-day Slovenia. Its imposing castle, now a regional museum, dates from medieval times, when it was a flourishing trade and crafts centre.

170. Relief of the Virgin and Child in the famous Gothic pilgrim church on nearby Ptujska gora, built around 1400.

171. Ptuj's Town Hall from the turn of the century is a 'newcomer' to this ancient town. Bypassed by the Southern Railway built in the mid-Nineteenth Century, Ptuj was then overshadowed economically by its northern rival, Maribor, but retained its importance as a gateway to the Pannonian Plain.

172. *The town of Kočevje was twice destroyed by the Turks in the Fifteenth Century and badly damaged in the Second World War when the Allies bombed and obliterated in the fortress in the town centre.*

173. *A quiet corner of Skofja Loka lying below Lubnik Hill at the confluence of the Selška Sora and Poljanska Sora rivers.*

174. *In the alpine fashion, many older buildings in Slovenia are decorated with painted scenes.*

175. Kranj, mentioned as Carnia in the Seventh Century, is one of Slovenia's most important industrial centres. Strategically located on a ridge between the Sava and Korka rivers, it was already noted for its crafts in the Thirteenth Century.

176. *Picturesque Kanal in the deep valley gouged out by the River Soča is mentioned in the Twelfth Century as a fortified settlement. One of its towers now houses a gallery of the works of the eminent graphic artist Riko Debenjak. Kanal is one of the stations for the oldtime steam train that runs from Bled to Gorica.*

177. *The delightful coastal town of Piran (overleaf), dominated by the church of St George, is a maze of narrow streets, crowded onto a promontory. Tourism has now replaced fishing as the main source of income, though its many restaurants are still well supplied with seafood.*

178. *Piran's main square (opposite) with the statue of its most famous son, the composer and violin virtuoso, Giuseppe Tartini, who died in 1770.*

180. *The decorative style known as Venetian Gothic is a feature of many buildings along the Adriatic coast.*

179. *The Praetorian (Governor's) Palace from Venetian times in the walled town of Koper (Cappodistria), Slovenia's main port, which grew up at the head of the Istrian peninsula on what was originally an island, now joined to the mainland.*

*181. Izola (Isola), as its name suggests, is
another town that started out on an
island. Like Koper to the north and Piran
to the south, it has Roman roots, though
it must have kept a low profile since it
does not appear in records until 927.*

*182. An aerial view of Piran shows just
how skilfully its builders used every
square metre of the triangular headland.*

215

TOO MANY HUNGRY MOUTHS TO FEED on the farm did not merely foment rebellion, but forced a vigorous debate of various broader economic and social issues. Even before Martin Luther had posted his protest on the church door in 1517, the kings and emperors of Europe were themselves trying to impose changes in the relationship between serfs and feudal lords. Emperor Maximilian of Habsburg, the son of Frederic III, introduced the study of Roman Law at the University of Vienna in 1494, the second year of his reign, to counteract the power and influence of the rural nobility by educating clerks in the law. This launched the formation of an educated administrative class that in time facilitated the formation of central state authority.

This very worldly ruler liked to boast that he had been taught to speak Slovene by his Latin teacher Tomaž Prelokar from Celje who later became a bishop in Constanza. Also at the court was Jurij Slatkonja from Ljubljana who was the court choirmaster and composer and founded the chapel boys choir which was the forerunner of today's Vienna Boys Choir. He later became the first bishop of Vienna. To consolidate his rule Maximilian built more and more bishop's palaces and for this commissioned his Chancellor, architect Avgustin Prygl Tyfernus who came from Laško, as evident from the name. One of the new palaces was in the Upper Town in Ljubljana. Just how enterprising people from the Slovene lands, who obviously also used the language, were is exemplified by Sigismund Žiga Herbertstein. An envoy of the court, he relates how he used his knowledge of Slovene during peace negotiations in Sultan Suleiman the Magnificent's camp, and demonstrates his close acquaintance with Russia in his book *Rerum Moscovitarum commentarrii*. Then again, the philosopher Matija Hvale (Qualle) from Vače, who was the dean of the philosophy faculty, is another of Vienna's intellectual elite before, during and after the Reformation, who came from this land.

Great changes were taking place in farming. The new era brought improved techniques and new varieties of crops like buckwheat, which planted as the second crop increased overall yields, and maize (corn). These helped the peasant farmers to survive, since they were obliged to give part of their wheat to the feudal lords. Deforestation was on the increase to create more grazing land, produce charcoal as fuel for the iron foundries, and provide timber for construction and various crafts. In addition to cultivating their modest plots, many people eked out their meagre incomes by other activities, such as handicrafts (like the cottage industries of today) as well as transport services.

As the Habsburg Empire expanded into formerly Turkish-occupied Hungarian and Croatian territories and into the Banat region of the eastern Vojvodina Plain, new doors to the south and west were opening up for the Austrian Empire, bringing the entrepreneur new opportunities. As early as 1689, a Ljubljana merchant named Blaznik began trading with Belgrade, even before it was temporarily freed from Turkish rule (and occupied by the Austrians) in a brilliant military campaign led by Prince Eugene of Savoy in the Austro-Turkish war of 1716-1718. The regional opening up had a strong impact on economic and commercial trends in Slovene lands. The burgeoning of towns and the drive for freedom of movement infected the inhabitants there too. More and more candidates for secondary and higher education streamed towards Vienna, just like the chestnut and dry goods peddlers to this day. From 1450 to 1550, for example, there were about 33,000 students enrolled at university faculties there. A tenth of them came from Carniola and other Slovene lands, and the numbers climbed steadily in the coming years.

JUST LIKE WATER, WHICH PUSHES THROUGH BARRIERS and finds a way around or through rocks, goods trading broke down feudal and other borders, partly as a result of Habsburg trade and economic policies. The

183. Novo Mesto (New Town), the regional centre of Dolenjska, a lush green region of rolling vineyards and forests, was not 'new' even at the beginning of the Fifteenth Century when it got its name. Rudolf IV had founded it only some fifty years earlier. But the site had been settled continuously since 100 BC. A rich treasure-trove of archaeological finds recounts the lives of previous residents – Illyrian, Celtic and the Latobe tribes, and later Romans all of whom would doubtless have liked to stay. In more recent centuries the Ottoman incursions prevented gentle, friendly Dolenjska developing faster than the more mountainous and forbidding Gorenjska to the north. Nowadays the path to growth is unhindered.

city port of Trieste demanded freedom of the seas as early as 1513. But it took another two hundred years to win because of the Venetians, the Turks, the *Uskoki* pirates operating from the Dalmatian town of Senj, and other vested interests. Only in 1719 did were Trieste and Rijeka (Fiume) granted the special status of free ports by Emperor Charles VI. This gave a major boost to trade in wine and timber, exports of craft products, minerals, textiles and metal goods, and exotic fruits and other goods from European overseas colonies began to flow in. There was also huge traffic in sea salt through these ports, as well as along the northern Adriatic coast, amounting to more than 3,500 tons a year. As in the case of the Idrija mercury mine, tax officials in Vienna took full advantage of the great demand and declared the production and sale of salt a state monopoly.

In those times, the economy of the Karst became closely linked with the transport of goods to and from the Adriatic ports which provides the setting for the story of Martin Krpan. This strong and simple, but quick-witted smuggler from the village of Vrh was immortalised in a realistic folk-tale by Fran Levstik (1831-1887): Once upon a time, when the Emperor was travelling through the Karst region, his carriage came to a halt in front of Martin Krpan and his pony, laden with smuggled salt. To avoid detection and trouble, the brawny Krpan scooped up his pony with the load and carried it to the side of the road to make way for the carriage. He said he was transporting a mill-stone (a metaphor for the burden borne by Krpan and all Slovenes). Impressed by the man's strength, the Emperor later invited him to Vienna to fight with the giant Brdavs and defend the honour of the Empire.

This story draws upon an ancient Slovene folk-tale about the defeat of the wicked giant Pegam by the good Lambergar, a theme found all the world over. Another source may have been the popular tale about the folk hero Peter Klepec from Čabar (now in Croatia), who was considered by all to be a coward until one day an inner voice told him he could accomplish anything if his desire was strong enough. After proving his strength to all and sundry, Klepec went off to Vienna, where he defeated a Turkish champion and then uprooted a tree and used it like a broom to sweep away all the Turks who set upon him. Having saved the Emperor, he left for home, very pleased with himself.

Levstik used Martin Krpan as a model of the resourcefulness, quick wit and native cunning of the ordinary Slovene and to castigate the flatterers and hypocrites surrounding the Emperor. He went so far as to point to 'the eternal ingratitude shown by the Emperor and the nobility towards the hard-working and great-hearted common Slovene people'.

At the same time, Levstik endeavoured to apply his principle that 'one should always write from the standpoint of a simple man, so that he can understand'. The tale of Martin Krpan, published in 1858, became immensely popular and influential, entering into the national mythology. However, in the era of national awakening, some practical Slovenes attacked Levstik for portraying Krpan as 'a typical Slovene' who soon became bored with Viennese society and returned to his village satisfied with only a imperial permit that legalised smuggling. They argued that 'hard-working, resourceful, reliable and loyal' Slovenes should be more ambitious and make proper use of their abilities in the service of the Empire.

Even before they had been declared free ports, systematic plans to improve transportation through the Trieste and Rijeka hinterland were drawn up and some work actually carried out. Bridges were built and the roads improved to speed up goods traffic by bypassing the long, slow routes along meandering rivers and ferried crossings. The Empire's principal thoroughfare now led from Vienna through Ljubljana and south-east to Trieste and Rijeka. The road from Ljubljana over the Ljubelj/Loibel pass, through Klagenfurt and beyond across the Alps to the north, was also gaining in importance. Major waterways flowing to the east were also a matter of great interest, as a way of facilitating trade with the Ottoman Empire: hindrances to traffic on the Sava River started to be cleared, for instance. But the advent of the railway, particularly the Southern Railway connecting the three largest towns in Slovenia with Vienna and the Adriatic ports, superseded all other modes of transport in significance in the middle of the Nineteenth Century.

THE GREAT EXPECTATIONS underlying all these developments had in many ways been inaugurated by the philosophers of the Age of Enlightenment. Man could discover the truth simply by virtue of his intellect. He could shed light in the darkness of ignorance and prejudice, the philosophers taught. It was a battle for freedom of thought and tolerance. Everyone, they argued, should be equal before the law. Legislative power should rest with the people, executive power should be exercised by the designated leader, and the judiciary should remain independent of both.

Several centuries have passed since those sublime visions, and instead of victories for the intellect they have brought absurd controversies and terrible crimes, committed all too often in the name of ideologies and `ideals'. Still, whilst we wait for King Matjaž, or with Vladimir and Estragon for Beckett's Godot, we should suspend judgement and take a look at the wonderful legacy the Enlightenment left Slovenia.

These philosophical ideas inspired many thinkers who were destined to settle in Ljubljana or elsewhere in Slovenia. A pioneer was Johann Ludwig Schoenleben (1618-1681). Descended from a family of German settlers, he became dean of the Ljubljana diocese and produced 38 books, the most outstanding of which is his unfinished history of Carniola. At his bequest, his work was continued by Johann Weichard Valvasor, born in Ljubljana to an Italian family that had immigrated to Carniola. Valvasor expanded Shoenleben's original concept and published four huge volumes entitled *Die Ehre*

Metlika, on the border with Croatia, which often suffered from Turkish attacks.

des Herzogthums Krain (The Glory of the Dutchy of Carniola) in 1689. This vast work contained hundreds of copperplate engravings of towns, monasteries, castles and a natural sites. The illustrations were accompanied by an equally copius text describing these places, the everyday lives of the populace, their language and national characteristics. A soldier, inventor, scientist, and social historian, Valvasor was made a fellow of the Royal Society in London.

Just a few years after Valvasor's death, a group of intellectuals, laymen and clergy founded the learned society, *Academia Operosorum Labacensium,* in Ljubljana. Its objective was to organise scientific work and give direction in the fields of theology, law, philosophy and medicine. Lawyer and composer Johann Bertold Hoffern was so enthused that he founded the *Academia Philharmonicorum* (Philharmonic Academy), the predecessor of the Slovenian Philharmonia, that very same year, 1701.

The *Academia Operosorum* has left an important, lasting monument in Ljubljana: the Baroque style. Under its influence many of the old Gothic churches made way for buildings in the new style or underwent a Baroque face-lift. Besides architecture, the fashion also prevailed in painting and sculpture. The organic unity of Ljubljana Baroque owes a great deal to a rising Italian influence, and the Operosorum elite who were mostly educated in Italy. Moreover, at that time, an increasing number of Italian artists were coming to live and work in Slovenia.

Energetic Maria Theresa (1740-1780), the Austrian Empress whose political credo was 'enlightened absolutism', encouraged the Enlightenment movement. To finance the strong army she considered essential, she fostered the development of the economy and formulated a taxation policy. Maria Theresa was convinced that there could be no real progress without education. In a remarkably short time, the dynamic Empress, and later her even more energetic son, the 'enlightened despot' Joseph II (1741-1790), created a powerful centralised system of government to which the whole society, including the church, was subordinated.

Realizing that the state, or the central government, could only boost taxation revenues by curtailing the exploitation of the peasants by the nobility, Maria Theresa started to restrict the dues collected by the feudal landowners. This policy was carried even further in the reign of Emperor Joseph II. The children of peasant families were encouraged to attend school and farmers were allowed to move freely and work in various craft and other industries. Compulsory service to the local feudal nobility was abolished, and the peasantry was no longer required to obtain permission to marry from their lords. Amongst the reformers of this epoch, Blaž Kumerdej deserves special mention for his 1772 Memorandum to the Empress Maria Theresa, suggesting the introduction of Sunday schools. Within two years, in 1774, the General School Reform was instituted, making elementary schooling obligatory throughout the Empire.

The second half of the Eighteenth Century also brought a number of important civil engineering projects, including land reclamation and drainage schemes. A canal, first proposed by the Jesuit Gabriel Gruber, was excavated to drain the Ljubljana Barje marshes, which had once been a large lake and home, three and a half thousand years earlier, to the pile-dwelling culture. In the domain of agriculture, the 'enlightened' Habsburg government allocated the common pasture land of the parishes to the farmers so that it would be used more productively. Higher yielding varieties of fodder, such as red clover, and new breeds of livestock were introduced. The government promoted the introduction of the potato as a staple crop, distributing seed potatoes and giving financial incentives. Nevertheless, the Slovene peasants were rigidly set against this 'new-fangled weed'. It is probably from the days of the 'potato resistance' that we have the folk saying: 'The dumbest farmer has the fattest potato'. A century was to pass before the conservative peasants took the 'risk' of having a good crop of potatoes. Yet, in time, the unwanted potato became the number-one crop in Slovenia and, along with bread, the main food in the national diet. These days, about fourteen per cent of all arable land is used for growing potatoes, and a quite different expression: 'he has potatoes', is used when things are going well for someone.

A critical part in the advancement of farming techniques was played by the Association for the Improvement of Farming and Useful Arts. Later called the Farmers' Society, it published popular scientific works, organised farm trials, gave awards for successful farming projects, helped introduce new varieties of crops and livestock, and promoted bee-keeping and hop-growing. Stables and barns of solid materials started to appear on the farms; the wooden houses gave way to dwellings of stone and, more and more, brick.

While the reforms of Maria Theresa and Joseph II in many respects strengthened the powers of the central government, there was a concurrent decentralisation with the institution of administrative districts and local government. The abolition or restriction of many of the administrative powers of the landed classes facilitated this process of devolution. Official posts were increasingly taken over by trained staff from the ranks of the minor landowners and the ordinary townsfolk.

The descendants of the serfs were at last making their way up the ladder.

Tinsmith.

THE NATIONAL AWAKENING MOVEMENT attracted a widening circle of educated people. Besides members of the clergy, they were mostly the educated sons of peasants who had remained close to the common people in both social status and wealth. One gathering place of the emergent Slovene intelligentsia was the home of Baron Žiga Zois. Born of a wealthy Italian father and a Slovene mother, Zois became the richest man in the land. With his breadth of vision and his rich library, he was a source of inspiration for a wide circle of national `awakeners', many of them proto-economic liberals, as well as Freemasons. A whole phalanx of 'enlightened' clergymen (Blaž Kumerdej, Ožbalt Gutsman, Jurij Japelj, Marko Pohlin, Valentin Vodnik, to name but a few) helped advance education, the standardisation and teaching of Slovene, collection and translation of the oral literature in order to promote the neglected language which was an embarrassment to many. Besides the clergy, there were many others in this circle.

Particularly fruitful and all-round in their contributions were Anton Tomaž Linhart, municipal school inspector for Ljubljana and Valentin Vodnik, a poet and journalist who was the founder of the first Slovene newspaper. Linhart, something of a Renaissance man, was the pioneer of Slovene drama, penning two comedies, *Županova Micka* (The Župan's Micka, 1789) and *Ta veseli dan ali Matiček se ženi* (This Merry Day or Matiček's Getting Married, 1790), which were patterned on German and French models. Together with his Freemason friends, he established the Friends of the Theatre Society. The destiny of Matiček resembled that of Beaumarchais' Figaro's Wedding: the censors prohibited its presentation in Slovene lands right up to 1848.

However, Linhart became even better known as a historian, thanks to his extensive work: *Poskus zgodovine Kranjske in drugih južnih Slovanov v Avstriji* (Essay on the History of Carniola and Other Southern Slavs in Austria), originally published in German in two volumes in 1789 and 1791. Because it deals with the history of the scattered Slovene people as a whole, this work has been called 'the most important cultural act of the Slovene national awakening in the Eighteenth Century'.

Many scientists and physicians came to Slovenia because of Idrija, the town that had opened the door on the new age for the whole country. An eminent Slovene from those times was Jurij Vega, whose logarithmic tables gained renown and who was lauded as the best mathematician in the Habsburg Empire.

BY THE END OF THE EIGHTEENTH CENTURY, the Slovene `ethnic amalgam' had come under the pressures of agitated tectonic masses around it. A new mass with very specific internal dynamics had emerged in the southeast. Austria had succeeded in fomenting revolt amongst the subjugated Croats, Serbs and Montenegrins following the expulsion of the Turks from Belgrade in 1688. A new political force was taking shape there that was of particular interest to Russia in its eagerness to acquire as much Ottoman territory as possible, and especially an outlet to the Mediterranean Sea. Other Slav nations within the Austro-Hungarian Empire took heed of the rebellious Serbs across the border, and similarly began to seek allies against their own rulers. Slavic Russia was adept in fomenting such ambitious. Both the Russian and Austrian imperial powers displayed exceptional talent and expended considerable money on winning over rebel leaders and governments, and actively encouraging coups to change them.

On the other side of the Atlantic, an independent America was proclaimed in 1776. Despite its remoteness, this event weakened England and bolstered the libertarian spirit in France and the whole of the Old World. At the same time it opened up new trading opportunities and an outlet for Europe's `superfluous' population. Then, in 1789 the fall of the Bastille marked the triumph of the French revolution, the virtual end of the 'divine right of kings' and the institution of an elected parliament. However, the achievements of Maria Theresa and her son Joseph II in the Habsburg Empire, inspired by the Enlightenment and based on gradual economic, social, political and cultural reforms rather than the guillotine and arbitrary decrees, were

in many ways more effective.

The beheading of Louis XVI in 1793 shocked the monarchs of Europe who joined forces against the French Republic. The ensuing battles brought to prominence a little Corporal, Napoleon Bonaparte, who became the 'bogeyman' of Europe, with the exception of Slovene lands. Still standing to this day in a beautiful corner of Ljubljana is a rare, if not unique outside of France, statue dedicated to this self-made emperor. Its erection in 1929 was somewhat belated, but the idea came straight from the heart.

A WIND OF CHANGE had swept through the Austrian Provinces all the way from France. It seemed to be blowing Europe's revolving door off its hinges. The Jacobins and their revolutionary dictatorship in France struck fear in hearts around Europe. The Austrian court, already dubious about the reforms of Maria Theresa and Joseph II, started to revise them one by one. In 1793, a special police ministry was established within the Austrian Empire and immediately became the single most important organ of government. This move proved to be very prescient: no government anywhere has since been able to do without a similar institution. Another windbreak was the imposition of censorship to control the importation of 'subversive' literature. Many works by Voltaire, Kant, Herder and Goethe were prohibited, as were Shakespeare's Hamlet and King Lear, for they portrayed rulers in a poor light. In general, any piece was beyond the pale if it cast a noble higher in rank than a baron as a negative character.

Napoleon's army set foot on Slovene territory first in 1791 and then again in 1805 during the Franco-Austrian War. On both occasions the visits were very brief and quickly ended in truces and retreat. However, the third French occupation was longer lasting, from 1809 to 1814. After taking Dalmatia and what was formerly Venetian Istria in 1805, they went on to conquer the remaining parts of Istria, the territory around Gorica, the port of Trieste, the western part of Carinthia, all of Carniola, and Croatian lands south of the Sava River. In 1809, Napoleon formed the Illyrian Provinces, with Ljubljana as the

Ljubljana, the capital of Slovenia, copperplate engraving from 'The Glory of the Duchy of Carniola' by J. W. Valvasor (1689)

capital. (The name came from the common fallacy that the people living in these regions were descendants of the ancient Illyrians, something modern science has not been able to confirm.) So as not to antagonise the local feudal overlords the expected Revolutionary reforms were implemented only slowly and very cautiously. Nonetheless, by unifying the judiciary the French made all citizens equal before the law and the tax officials, which was a great step forward.

It is fondly recalled in Slovenia that four-grade elementary schools were established by the French and that pupils could then continue on to secondary schools in Ljubljana, Novo mesto, Idrija, Gorica, Koper, Trieste, Kranj, Postojna and Villach, or to vocational schools. A Central Academy was opened in Ljubljana, providing study in philosophy, medicine, law, technical sciences and theology for some three hundred, mainly theological, students. Since the language of instruction in the new schools was Slovene, Valentin Vodnik, a headmaster and supervisor general of schools, wrote a number of Slovene textbooks. Vodnik was so enthusiastic about the French reforms that he wrote a poem entitled *Ilirija oživljena* (Illyria Revived) as an ode to his homeland, liberty, and Napoleon Bonaparte. This is not surprising, for less than five years of French rule brought more benefits to the Slovene lands than the whole of the previous century.

BEHIND THE FACADE OF ENLIGNTENMENT were, of course, Napoleon's strategic plans. By forming the Illyrian Provinces and taking control of the Adriatic ports, he had blocked the Austrian Empire's outlet to the sea and effectively cut off links to its ally, Britain. The entire area was also intended to serve as a springboard for conquest of the Balkans and to advance further towards the Near East and Asia, thereby securing overland trade routes to Turkey. At one and the same time, Napoleon was also contriving to hasten the demise of the Ottoman Empire. Even before he had established the Illyrian Provinces, he had made contact with Karadjordje ('Black George') Petrović, the leader of the Serbian insurgence. Napoleon was aiming to destroy the Ottoman empire in the cheapest way, with the blood of people striving for freedom, in exactly the same way as Austria and Russia.

The great powers of the time willingly gave financial and other support to foster national awakening in the south-east. Liaison between Vienna and Serbia was assisted by Slovenes such as Jernej Kopitar, France Miklošič, and other Slavic linguists, historians and ethnologists who held influential positions in the imperial administration. Nonetheless, Serbia's nearly five centuries-long ties to Turkey, albeit by subjugation, inevitably engendered common interests and stereotypes. One thing they shared was an antagonism towards the *Latins*, and for the Roman Catholic Church in particular. Just how deep were the economic and religious differences between the southeastern and northwestern parts of this broad region was only fully appreciated in the Twentieth Century.

TAMING EVERY AGGRESSOR PROMPTLY was the task the victorious nations set themselves after the final defeat of Napoleon. At the Congress of Vienna (1814-1815), where the devout Tsar Alexander I cut such an impressive figure, the leading European states debated how to re-establish the balance of power Napoleon had disrupted, and how to check the spread of revolutionary ideas across the continent. In 1815 Austrian Emperor Francis I, Tsar Alexander I and King Frederick William III of Prussia jointly declared that they would 'live and rule in a caring, peaceable and righteousness manner and in accordance with the commandments of the true religion'. This 'Holy

186. A fresh, bright winter's day. Sun, glittering snow and a gentle breeze. Who could resist going back up to the top of the mountain, no matter how brief the delight?

187. In alpine skiing the legendary Tine Mule, Matevž Lukanc and Janko Štefet, have been joined by Bojan Križaj, the first Slovene to win the World Cup medal, Boris Strel, who won the first Olympic medal, Mateja Svet, Rok Petrovič and others.

188. The latest, brilliant generation of downhill skiers includes Alenka Dovžan, Katja Koren and Urška Hrovat, and Jure Košir and others. The Slovenes have produced excellent ski jumpers – first Janez Polde and Rudi Finžgar, then Primož Ulaga, Miran Tepeš, and France Petek, who in 1991 became the first world champion. Another star, Primož Peterka has risen recently.

189. In the between-war period gymnasts won a total of 8 Olympic medals and the top ski discipline was cross-country. Franc Smolej of Jesenice ranked amongst the fastest cross-country skiers in the world. Along with Olympic medal winner, Leon Štukelj (celebrated by the world at the last Olympic Games as oldest living champion) was one of the nation's most successful sportsmen of that time.

190. *What does it feel like to mount the prize-winners' podium? Merely watching one of 'our' competitors win first place is a great enough joy.*

191. Man's quests and achievements are serving more and more for pleasure-taking under the open skies.

192. Mountain biking has very rapidly
won a great following that is even taking
it across crystalline crests.

193. Horse-riding is a fine, elegant sport, probably because it is not exactly inexpensive. The feats of the Lipica equestrian team astride their famous white horses are dazzling.

*194. Most people are content to merely
watch riding competitions from the
stands, with a winning betting slip in
their pocket, preferably.*

195. Skiing is the top favourite in Slovenia, despite the jams on the snow-covered roads to the slopes.

196. The Kanin Ski Centre right on the Italian border is very popular because the season lasts the longest there. A joint Slovenian-Italian-Austrian bid is being made to organise the Winter Olympics in 2006 in this broad area.

197. –198. Kayaking and white-water canoeing are strong sports in Slovenia, like many others. International awards have been won in both, as well as in swimming, parachuting, rowing, skittles, bowls, cycling and motor sports. Britta Bilač is a European champion in high jump, Brigita Bukovec is a medallist in hurdling, Gregor Cankar won gold at the world youth championship in the long jump, marksman Rajmond Debevc has been world champion for some years…

Alliance' was later joined by almost every European country and met at three further congresses to define more precisely this fundamental programme. One of these congresses was held in Ljubljana in 1821. The Austrian Chancellor, Prince Metternich, had planned to stage it at Gorica, because of the more agreeable climate, but because of the press of numbers he had to move it to Ljubljana.

The imperial government in Vienna decided to retain the Illyrian Provinces as they had been under French administration. The idea was mooted of forming an Illyrian Kingdom within the Empire, to encompass Carniola, Carinthia, the Gorica district, Trieste, Istria and the Karlovac region in Croatia, but nothing came of this. Not many Slovenes were very enthusiastic about the Illyrian concept because it presumed a common Southern Slav culture and language. The Illyrian Movement persisted in Croatia for a time until it was quashed by the Hungarian nobility, as were demands by the Southern Slavs for trilateral organisation of the Empire.

Metternich, the arch politician, kept under tight control the ever-recurring demands for reform that persisted for decades. First he cracked down on all nationalist political movements, quite correctly perceiving them as a threat to the monarchy and the integrity of the Empire. By such repressive measures Europe's rulers and statesmen managed to secure for the Old Continent a period of relative peace, marked by economic growth, expanding trade, improving communications, and new markets around the globe. All of which, in their turn, helped undermine the surviving feudal privileges.

1848 started with a spring just like every other year. But this particular one has gone down in history as the Spring of Nations.

199. Enthusiasm for sport has grown since sportsmen and sportswomen began representing their own country, Slovenia. Basketball has long been very popular. In his time Ivo Daneau was the best amateur basketball player in the world. In 1971, Ljubljana hosted the world basketball championship, and prior to that the world table tennis championship. The Tivoli stadium has been the stage for the top ice hockey players, gymnasts, ice skaters, weight-lifters and bowlers ... in short – just about everything.

AND WHAT ABOUT TOMORROW?

WAS INDEPENDENCE TOO EARLY OR TOO LATE? This is a dilemma that only future generations can hope to settle. It is clear now, however, that the final step on the journey from the United Slovenia Programme to a sovereign state was unavoidable under the circumstances that prevailed.

The Republic of Slovenia was attacked just a few hours after the declaration of independence on the square in front of the Parliament in the evening of 26 June 1991. The Yugoslav Peoples Army (YPA), an unpredictable colossus, which in the age of *detente* stood like a dinosaur amongst the tulips, launched an invasion. The young nation resisted in a fashion worthy of its rebellious reputation and the unflinching resourcefulness of a David wrestling with Goliath.

The ten days of hostilities thankfully led to few casualties: 76 people died, of whom 29 were nationals, 36 YPA soldiers, and 11 foreigners. After just a few days of skirmishes followed by a tense stand-off, the Yugoslav Army bowed to international pressures and agreed to a cease-fire, avowing: 'If the Slovenes don't want us, we will go of our own free will.'

Such surprising probity of the YPA, on the heels of its arrogance and readiness to use force in the dying years of the former-Yugoslavia, had its explanations. The fundamental reason was simply that it had failed to intimidate and paralyse the provident Slovenes by swift policing action and destructive force. Instead, it had met with whole-hearted mass resistance that clearly signalled a readiness for long-term guerrilla warfare in the best Partisan traditions of the Second World War. Moreover, it was obvious that sooner or later the Slovenes would appeal to NATO.

Other reasons for the Yugoslav Army's sudden conciliation are disclosed by YPA documents that should interest the Hague War Crimes Tribunal. These reveal that the army had begun to plan its entrenchment along a line east of Slovenia, from Virovitica-Karlovac-Karlobag in Croatia, long ago, just after the death of President Tito. This line coincided with the long-vaunted western frontier of Greater Serbia, revived once again by the nationalist lobby in the 1986 Memorandum drawn up by the Serbian Academy of Sciences and Arts. It also uncannily co-relates with the fifty-fifty, East-West division of former-Yugoslavia agreed upon by the Super Powers after the Second World War. With the collapse of communism, however, matters became complicated.

By abandoning their garrisons and withdrawing from Slovenia entirely, the Serb-controlled YPA astutely averted the threat of a likely NATO intervention, in view of the proximity of the Italian and Austrian borders. With independent Slovenia as a buffer between it and the theatres of war in Croatia and Bosnia-Herzegovina, NATO was relieved of the necessity to intervene directly. Lucky Slovenia thus thankfully faded from the spotlights.

ONE JULY DAY AT LJUBLJANA RAILWAY STATION, the last composition of the Ljubljana-Belgrade train was shunted into the sidings at the end of its last 600-kilometre trip from Belgrade. This blue hotel on wheels, which belonged to Slovenian Railways, had become quite famous in the final decades of former-Yugoslavia. In spite of innumerable declarations of decentralisation, it was still necessary to travel to Belgrade for every little thing. Ticket sales were brisk as municipal, republican, federal, party and self-management bureaucrats vied for them. There were numerous daily air connections and fairly good road connections. Still, it was usually difficult to get a seat. Travelling in the plush Pullman carriages and saloon cars carried a certain prestige, like President Tito's Blue Train that had carried him on his tours of the country.

But all the comings and goings abruptly ceased on that July day. It is difficult to understand how all those vital journeys suddenly became unnecessary, or why they had not stopped earlier. In truth, most of the trips to Belgrade resembled the folklore visits of Peter Klepec and Martin Krpan to Vienna - quick and short. Mostly they were day-trips ending with a dash to catch the first afternoon train and idle away the journey playing endless games of cards.

Over the years, the number of Slovenes residing in Belgrade had been shrinking steadily. The 1981 census recorded only 6,005 or half the number of ten years previously. By the 1991 census there were a mere 3,628, most of whom were long-timers who had settled there in the early post-Second World War period. So on that July day in 1991, when the long empty train slipped into Ljubljana, it was almost as if Lepa Vida (Lovely Vida), a figure from Slovene folklore, was stepping down from the last of the carriages.

A TIME OF UNCERTAINTY opened even while the Yugoslav Army forces waited to complete their withdrawal and go to battle in Croatia and Bosnia-Herzegovina. Slovenia next faced hard struggles on another front. The economic crisis that had been raging for years was exacerbating daily. By 1990, industrial production had fallen all together by more than an eighth after a five-year decline. It was obvious that the trend would not relent. Whereas in 1987 the active work-force numbered 850,000 and unemployment was 1.7 per cent, by 1990 it had reached 6 per cent, and jumped to an alarming 15 per cent by 1993.

Krško, engraving from the late Seventeenth Century.

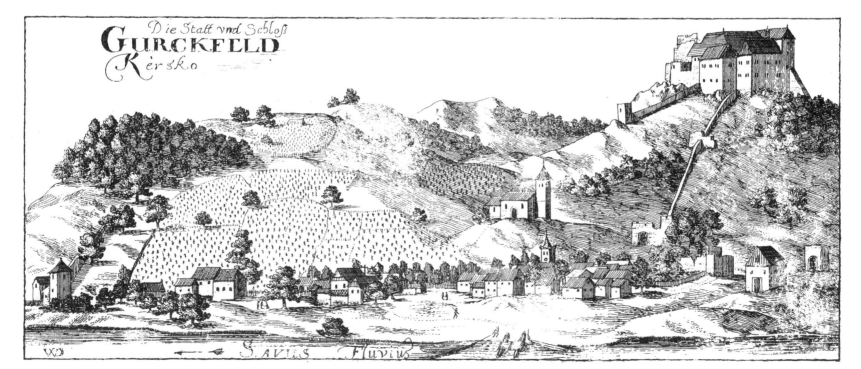

243

In the three years following the declaration of independence, Slovenia's level of production, total number employed and the national GDP fell to 1970 levels (in 1994, per capita GDP dropped to 6,071 US dollars, as against 8,643 US dollars in 1990). If this statistic were not enough to send a cold shiver down the spine, there were other facts to consider. In the 1970s Slovenia had over-employment: a remarkable 44 per cent of the population were economically active. But when the country stepped into independence, the percentage of the population at or above pensionable age was higher than anywhere else in Europe. When the total number of pensioners is added to the estimated quarter of a million unemployed, all of whom need to be supported, it is clear that Slovenia with its population of two million faced economic problems of enormous proportions. Nevertheless, by astute taxation and incomes policies the 1994 budget was kept in balance, which boded well for the future.

THE STARTING POINT for planning the future was the data collected in the regular ten-year census in 1991. Permanent residents in Slovenia numbered 1,965,986. Population density was 97.1 per square kilometre, or higher than in the neighbouring Croatia (85) and Austria (94), but lower than in Hungary (111) and Italy (189). In 1991, 87.84 per cent of the population were Slovenes, compared to 90.52 ten years previously, and 95.65 per cent in 1961. The remainder were Croats (23 per cent), Serbs (20), Muslim (11), Hungarians (3.5), Italians (1.3), and other smaller minorities.

In 1991 Slovenia's population was older on average than in almost all the OECD countries, with the exception of Australia, Canada, Iceland, Ireland, Turkey, New Zealand and the USA. By the end of 1993, it had even aged a little more: the 0-15 year age group had declined by 1.5 per cent in two years to only 19 per cent. At the other end of the scale, there was almost a one per cent increase in the number of people over 65. In 1961 the average life expectancy of males was calculated at 66.1 years. Since then improvements in living standards have raised it to 69.5 for men, and from 71.9 to 77.4 years for women. Life expectancy is thus only slightly below the average in Europe (75), although noticeably lower than the averages in northern, southern and western Europe, as well as in the USA and Canada.

HOW OLD WILL LEPA VIDA GET? This question naturally springs to mind for all those who know the lady. Lepa Vida (Lovely Vida) had lived among the people for centuries before being officially introduced in 1830 by the nation's greatest poet, France Prešern. He took his inspiration from a 'ballad sung by the people of Carniola' on the ancient theme of a kidnapped wife and mother. A century later, literary historian and ethnologist Ivan Grafenauer delved into the reasons why this woman, who had been lured abroad and then drawn back home by a longing for all she had left behind, had become so deeply inscribed in the folk memory.

Grafenauer discovered several different versions of the story in various sources, all sharing the basic theme of a woman who is carried abroad by a 'pagan' or 'unbeliever' (in short, a 'foreigner'). In one version a 'negro' seizes her and makes her his slave. In another she is a wet-nurse in a Spanish castle where she is protected from abuse by the Spanish queen herself. This is reminiscent of the hundreds of 'Alexandrian' women from the Primorska region who not so long ago used to be sent to work as nannies and wet-nurses in Egypt. In a third version, she becomes a paramour or a wife in a foreign country. But each time she succeeds, returning wealthy to take her son away to her new home.

The Lepa Vida theme dates back to the Thirteenth Century folk songs, and is an allegory about life in the Slovene lands. It recounts feelings of guilt or regret about fleeing from the hardships of poverty to a richer and more developed, and non-Slovene, place as well as accusations of desertion, even treachery. There were, in fact, countless such 'defections' to Austrian lands or the coastal towns where ethnic Germans or Italians dominated every aspect of life. In these places, moreover, opposition to a separate Slovene culture and identity was the strongest.

Another version of the story may yet appear, with Lepa Vida coming home on that day in July 1991 on the last Belgrade - Ljubljana train after seventy-two years in Yugoslavia and a fifty-year liaison with Communism. After all, there have been at least fifty variations of the poem written so far, even by some by the most distinguished Slovenian literary figures, and it has inspired numerous musical works, ballets and paintings.

SLOVENIA'S RICH ARTISTIC AND LITERARY OUTPUT cannot easily be catalogued here by artist or author, period and genre. In 1991 alone, 422 works of literature were published in Slovenia, of which 249 were new titles, and in 1992 there were 277 new works out of 337 published titles. Only Austria, Denmark, Finland, Germany, Luxembourg, Spain, Sweden and Switzerland publish more titles per capita. In the number of newspapers and magazines published and their circulation per thousand inhabitants, Slovenia was well ahead of the other republics of the former Yugoslavia, but it is still well down in European rankings.

The range of publications is enriched by the Italian and Hungarian ethnic minorities, as well as the Slovene Diaspora living in Argentina, the USA, Canada and Australia. Since the political barriers to co-operation with the homeland have been removed publication and translation of Slovene books abroad will probably increase so that Slovene literature can be appreciated more widely.

AN AFFINITY FOR MUSIC has been demonstrated since the distant past. Slovenes had their own folk songs, and specific terms for 'song' and 'singing' in the Sixth Century. Many musical talents went abroad. At the end of the Fourteenth Century, Balthasar Praspergius from Mozirje was teaching music at the University of Basel, and Jurij Slatkonja became renowned as court choirmaster and bishop in Vienna, and played an important role in bringing Dutch polyphony to central Europe. A major contribution was also made by Jacob Gallus Carniolus (1550-1591), one of the greatest European composers of the Sixteenth Century. Ljubljana acquired its Academia Philharmonicorum, together with its orchestra and choir, in 1701. It is not surprising, then, that the Slovenes long ago gained a reputation for being strongly musically-inclined. Their passion for singing is reflected in the popular expression: 'Two Slovenes - a choir'. The Hungarians have a saying: 'Two Slovenes sing in four voices'.

Besides renowned soloists, two opera companies, permanent symphonic orchestras, numerous choirs, the country has established instrumental ensembles too numerous to mention here. Many national and international music festivals and contests are held, which has helped establish the reputation of Slovenian musicians and singers abroad.

The theatre is another passion. There are as many as eight professional theatres and numerous children's, youth, amateur and experimental companies. Some have performed all over the world and received enthusiastic reviews. As with music, the international festivals held in Slovenia enhance their reputation abroad, as well as foster strong public interest in theatre.

DELIGHT IN THE ARTS would seem to go back to prehistoric times. Ornamentation can be found on Neolithic pottery. The human-shaped idol that is attributed to the pile-dwelling culture of the Ljubljana Barje marshes, is a remarkable statuette bearing clothing that appears quite modern to the casual observer. The ancient Vače situla with its elegant, stylised figures has inevitably attracted contemporary designers and souvenir-makers. The same is the case with numerous remarkable specimens of Celtic and Roman culture and civilisation found on this territory.

After a brief period of Socialist Realism which was abandoned in the early 1950s, there was a great upsurge in all forms of artistic activity in Slovenia. The highest international reputation has been achieved in the graphic arts largely due to the graphic schools of Riko Debenjak and Božidar Jakac and, above all, to Slovenia's International Graphic Arts Biennial, which attracts leading artists from around the world. Another major event is the International Biennial of Industrial Design.

With intellectual and socio-political bonds loosened now a huge amount of creative and innovative energy is being released. Post-modern architects are taking their place alongside the early Twentieth-century masters, such as architects and designers Jože Plečnik and Maks Fabiani. Architecture and design have traditionally been highly valued in Slovenia. They will hopefully be turned to effective use in tackling environmental and urban problems, which are likely to become more pressing in the future. Slovenian towns are steadily gaining a clearly distinctive character. Ljubljana seems to be taking the lead in this respect and is quite 'chic' with its attractive blend of modern, Baroque and other architectural styles.

'DISSATISFIED AT HOME, THE CRANES FLY ACROSS THE SEA.' These lines from Prešern's *Lepa Vida* poem describe how and why Slovenes have scattered far and wide. Although they have their own country now, they will no doubt continue to be drawn abroad in quest of 'promised' lands.

In his preface to Drago Medved's book *Slovenski Dunaj* (Slovene Vienna), the mayor of Vienna, Helmut Zilk counts altogether about 40 deans and rectors of faculties, academies and institutes in Vienna who were of Slovene origin. Like similar books (Italian Vienna, Czech Vienna, etc.) it reviews how Slovenes have helped shape the city and observes that 'not seldom in historical events they were in the forefront and not on the margins'. To this day some of the streets bear the names of Slovenes who lived and worked there, such as the writer Ivan Cankar, mathematician and ballistics expert Jurij Vega, a peasant's son who rose to noble title, linguist Miklošič, architect Plečnik, and others. The fact that similar honours have not been recorded in Belgrade may be attributed to the fact that for the Slovenes the 'Yugoslav episode' was much shorter, and some other reasons.

In his book *The Slovenian Heritage* (1974), Dr Edward Gobetz, examines the contribution the Slovenes have made to America and the world at large. He is a professor of sociology and anthropology at Kent State University in Ohio, and founder of the Slovenian Research Centre in the USA. At the outset he relates the impact of Karantanian enthronement ceremony on Thomas Jefferson when he was drafting the American Declaration of Independence and his evaluation of it as 'a democratic ritual that has yet to be surpassed'. He identifies five generals, five admirals and five bishops including the missionary Frederik Baraga (1797 - 1868), whose visions and ideas on cultural pluralism were adopted by the US Congress one hundred and forty years later. Slovene Americans and their descendants have won election to Congress, as state governors and mayors. Several hundred have made their mark as university professors, judges, architects, writers, actors, singers, inventors and innovators. Thousands have become prosperous businessmen. Sometimes, like many other immigrant Americans, they adopted anglicised surnames for ease of pronunciation, but most remained close to their Slovene-American communities. It is a similar story for all those Slovene emigrants who went to Australia, Canada, northern and western Europe and elsewhere: a great many moved 'temporarily' seeking work and for one reason or another put down permanent roots.

Edward Gobetz and his associates have collected and published a wealth of other material on Slovenes and their descendants who have made their way to the top. People like Georg Leo von Caprivi (1831-1899), the son of a peasant from Koprivnik in Carniola, who followed Bismarck to become the second chancellor of Germany (1890 -1894) when it was one of the most powerful states in Europe. Dr Kurt von Schuschnigg (1897 -1977), who became Austrian chancellor after Dollfuss was murdered by the Nazis, was also aware of his Slovene origins: his family came from Gorica or Goritschach in Carinthia. His grandfather had moved to the town of Klagenfurt and became a grain merchant. Von Schuschnigg held the post of chancellor at a critical time in Austrian history, up to the arrival of Hitler's troops in 1938.

Outside of politics, Gobetz mentions Dr Marcus Anton Plenciz (Plenčič), who was born in 1705 at Solkan on the River Soča and studied

Vrhnika, copperplate engraving from 'The Glory of the Duchy of Carniola'. by J. W. Valvasor (1689)/

medicine at Padua. In 1762, Plenciz developed a theory on the causes of infectious diseases, some one hundred years before Louis Pasteur. For his scientific achievements, Maria Theresa elevated him to nobility and granted him estates. An Italian title was also conferred upon him. Another deserving mention is the unlucky Lovrenc Košir (Laurenz Koschier, 1840 - 1879), born near Škofja Loka, who developed the first postage stamp in 1835, although the official credit goes to the Englishman, Sir Rowland Hill. A great Slovene who did receive just acclaim was Frederik Pregl (1869-1930), a native of Ljubljana, who won the 1923 Nobel Prize for chemistry. Acknowledged as the 'father of micro-analysis', Professor Pregl bequeathed his laboratory to Ljubljana University.

Gobetz has an especially long list of ethnic Slovenes who made their name in various branches of technology. Among these are many from this century who studied in their homeland. The list includes such pioneers as Max Stupar from Metlika, who in 1909 built the first American aeroplane factory, the aeronautical engineers Žele, Raspet and Kisovec, the automobile designer of genius John Bucik, and many other engineers and managers in the automotive and electronic industries. The father of rocket science and space travel, Werner von Braun, has recounted that he had learnt most about human flight into space from two books published in 1929 by a Slovene named Herman Potočnik-Noordnung. Finally, there is Ronald Sega, whose family came from Loški Potok, who is a member of the American Space Shuttle crew, and flew into space in 1994.

WHERE AND HOW IN THE FUTURE? The young country has to answer these questions now as it stands at the cross-roads. Unquestionably it will be no easier now than in the past to keep all talented people at home within its 'narrow and constraining' borders. It is often argued that it has become even harder in modern times for small countries because the opportunities for personal advancement and achievement are too limited. The Slovenian economy is vulnerable and will be hard put to protect itself from pressures exerted by larger economies. Furthermore, Slovenians are only just learning how to run a country, the necessary infrastructure is lacking and they do not yet think or act in a statesmanlike way. Being confined to such a small area, beyond which the language is unknown, can have a claustrophobic effect on those who prefer to 'breathe with full lungs'. But communications can be greatly increased through radio and television, the Internet and publications in foreign languages. Borders can be softened, even eliminated, and international links strengthened, with sufficient government support.

The recovery and normal functioning of the economy has been rightly regarded as a matter of paramount importance. Besides finding new markets, the economy has had to undergo a very deep and fundamental post-communist transformation and restructuring. It was easy for Slovenia to be the 'finest fish in the Yugoslav pond' and quite frustrating to find its position 'in the ocean' was quite different. What is more, this change in relative rank has come in the midst of a steep decline in economic activity, employment and living standards.

The Institute of Macroeconomic Analysis and Development of Slovenia gathered a think-tank together to find the blue sky above the clouds and draw up a long-term plan. In October 1991, the first national currency, the tolar, was issued in one of the most important acts following the declaration of independence.

202. - 203. *Joco Balant is a tour-ski enthusiast and his picture shows 'there is nothing lovelier'. At Vršič you can even ski on top of traffic signs when the snow is right.*

204. The Partisans built the Franja hospital in a secret, narrow gorge to care for the war-wounded in the Second World War. Blanketed in snow, it is preserved as a memorial to freedom fighters.

205. Life moves on …

206. ... even fathers can be useful at times.

207. –208. Summers can be very hot and it is wonderful to just laze and fish, and not even notice that someone sits alone in the silence of an abandoned mill.

209. –210. Oh, the passion of the fisherman, the driving urge of the hunter, that gives no pause nor peace.

211. Rogaška Slatina (above), Slovenia's oldest and most famous spa, attracts many visitors from abroad. The names of spas usually include the words 'slatina' or 'toplice', which indicated whether they have cold or hot mineral springs.

212-216. Slovenia's spas offer recreation and medical treatment for various complaints and disorders, depending on the properties of the local mineral springs. Some people go just for a relaxing holiday and the excellent indoor and outdoor pools, as at Čateške toplice.

217, 218. Moravci spa (above) and Atomske toplice ('atomic hot springs') near Podčetrtek below Olimje Castle (left). There are fourteen spas in the country, most of them in the central and eastern regions.

219, 220. The young and healthy naturally prefer the sea to the spas. Slovenia's short coastline of 47 kilometres has both historic small towns and sophisticated resorts.

221. Those who find the sea too salty, too crowded or too warm, can cool off beneath an ice-cold highland waterfall or swim in one of the natural or artificial lakes.

222-226. The joy of carefree youth is reflected in the faces of these cheerful young people. Though the Slovenes have a reputation for thrift, most parents readily make financial sacrifices to buy their children the latest ski-ing equipment, pay for music lessons or provide them with computers.

227, 228. Courtship can begin young, down on the farm, and end in a shower of rice, to bring luck to the newly-weds. With their carefree youth behind them, young couples must work hard to buy or build their own home. Even before independence, private home-ownership was increasingly the norm in Slovenia.

229. Dante Alighieri is said to have visited the
Tolmin Gorge and the terror he experienced
supposedly inspired him when he was describing
Hell in the first book of his 'Divine Comedy'.

230. The virgin forests of Kočevje were the
bastion of the Partisans during World War II, but
also, at the war's end, the site of mass graves of
several thousand Slovenes who had willingly or
not fought on the side of the invaders.
A reconciliation ceremony was held in the forest
in 1990.

231, 232. Scenes from a dramatized version of Dante's 'Divine Comedy', staged as three separate performances by the talented young director Tomaž Pandur. Overcoming the language barrier, it won high praise from critics when performed abroad.

233. The central Slovene cultural centre, Cankarjev dom, in Ljubljana, where concerts, theatrical performances and all manner of other cultural events are held. It is named after Ivan Cankar, one of Slovenia's most eminent prose writers.

234. Interest in the arts can be gauged by the large number of visitors to exhibitions.

235. Like choirs, brass bands are a widespread form of popular music-making. On the professional level, there are several symphony orchestras, among them the Slovenian Philharmonic in Ljubljana, the successor of the Academia Philharmonicorum, founded in 1701.

236. The beauties and bounties left by the past in Slovenia are readily shared with everyone `from near and far'.
New ways are constantly being found to bring all the legacies, from the venerable manuscripts in the monasteries around the country to the magnificent works of art, closer to the visitor. One such initiative is holding an Early music festival in the Knights' Hall of the Brežice Castle, where the peerless acoustics and magnificent Seventeenth Century frescoes shown in Marko Turk's photograph provide a perfect setting.

237-239. Today, as three centuries ago, when the leading spirits of the Enlightenment in Ljubljana founded the Academia Operosorum and the forerunner of this library (opposite), much is expected of science and scholarship. But just as important are the skills of the country's craftsmen. High-quality glassware and wood products are long-established and important export articles.

240 – 241. *There is no room for pessimism, not with a child in your arms, or even better two: one for mum and one for dad, and two for the tax man one day. With accession to the European Union looming, this country, which has always been an intensive migration area, may have to make some adjustments.*

242. *Getting a piece of cake for everybody is the long term goal of the country as it battles to bring down unemployment, raise incomes, and the general standard of living.*

243. Lets hope for lots more bright and happy jubilees like this, the 850th anniversary of Ljubljana, when even the city's dragon got a cake.

244. ... and each year, the 'Kurenti' in their pagan costumes shall drive off winter and usher in the spring.

245-248. *A kaleidoscope of colourful scenes. Slovenes enjoy dressing up for carnivals and ceremonies although in every day life they prefer casual clothes. A quantity of these have been collected by an artist for one of the many 'happenings' that enliven the cultural scene.*

249. The names of all the meritorious will be engraved in gold. The pity is, of course, that only our descendants will have a chance to read them.

250.- 251. *Gay flags and banners egg on the competitors at an international ski race. Alpine skiing has brought the country the greatest number of medals and prizes of all the sports, and along with ski-jumping and jumpers like Primož Peterka, it is a source of great national pride.*

252. Let us not forget the lessons of constructor Janez Rožman and the father of Slovene sport, Stanko Bloudek, who opened the way to ski flying by building Planica where man first flew more than 100, and then 200 metres, on his own feet. They showed we can leap further.

The country is firmly set on a new course of parliamentary democracy, a multi-party political system, and pluralism of ownership. To get out of the economic crisis as quickly and smoothly as possible small and medium-scale enterprise, private and public, is being encouraged. In 1993 the statistics showed that the socialist enterprises, which still employed three-quarters of the workforce, only generated as much income as the private-sector firms. Moreover, per capita revenue was eight times higher in the private than in the public sector. Trend analysis indicates that unemployment, which rose to 15 per cent in the years following independence, should fall 13.2 per cent by the year 2002.

Slovenia's foreign exchange reserves are strong and are forecast to grow steadily thanks to a positive balance of trade. The export of both goods and services is expected to expand by some six per cent per year to the year 2000. Incomes and the fiscal needs of the social welfare system are expected to rise at a slower pace. It is predicted that growth will be highest in the service sectors (around five per cent), followed by industry (around three per cent) and agriculture which should achieve a growth rate of some 3.5 per cent in the last two years of the millennium.

The structure of the work force will also change markedly. In 1992 the smallest sectors in terms of labour force were agriculture, forestry and fisheries (12.1 per cent) followed by industry (40.6). The biggest sector was the tertiary or service sector, which employed 47.3 per cent. In line with all the other upward trends, it is predicted that per capita GNP will increase from 12.629 US dollars in 1997, to 14.772 US dollars by the year 2002. This is the conservative prognosis. More optimistic predictions say GNP could reach 15,953 US dollars by the end of the century.

People are much more complex and interesting than labour-force statistics, of course. Sociologist Gregor Tomc has studied the ethnic character of Slovenes. He found that some new features had been added to the archaic and traditional facets of the national character during the time spent in the Yugoslav state, especially the post-war socialist state. They had come to feel superior to the rest because of their greater level of employment and relative economic prosperity. (By the 1950s, Slovenia's GNP was already twice the Yugoslav average, and after 1975 substantially more than that.) This feeling of superiority, he claims, also disinclined them to involvement in politics. It was widely held (as in the West) that many of the people who did engage in it were not much good, and being a politician was not an entirely respectable occupation.

The political confrontation with Belgrade and 'Greater Serbia' protagonists encouraged various researches by Slovenes into the national character and identity. The year independence was declared also saw the publication of *Misli o slovenskem človeku* (Considerations on the Slovene), the life work of the eminent psychologist, Anton Trstenjak. Is a nation that thinks and writes a lot about its own character and soul indulging in some sort of collective narcissism? the book asks. Trstenjak's answer is: 'By doing so, a small nation is continually reinforcing its national identity.'

In a similar vein is a study by Janez Musek entitled Psychological Portrait of the Slovenes *Psihološki portret Slovenca* which seeks to extend Slovene self-knowledge by drawing on numerous foreign researches in addition to local studies. Thus he cites research by the British sociologists Barett and Eysenck in 1984 and concludes that the Slovenes are even more introverted than the British with their proverbial reticence and reserve, more inclined to psychotic states, and more eager to present themselves in

253. A hard climb upwards also faces the economy of the new state of Slovenia, but its people are determined it will prosper.

the best light possible. He goes on to deduce that British women are more pampered by their menfolk and so less emotionally stable than the Slovene. Slovene males are more self-centred, realistic and reserved, less sociable, think more carefully about their actions and have a greater sense of responsibility. The Slovenes are also cast as generally inhospitable, intolerant, aggressive, egoistic and suspicious, and compared with the British, more dogmatic and ambitious, and less willing to put up with being in a dependent or inferior position. In short, heaven preserve us from the Slovenes!

In the course of his deliberations, Musek decided that the stereotype of the Slovenes as closed and introverted is confirmed, but not the popular view that they are passive and humble. His assertion that the Slovene character displays more than enough aggression would seem to have been borne out six years later by the resistance shown during the ten-day war of independence. The people displayed a strong desire for independence and recognition. Other research into motivation at the work post reveals a lack of feeling for co-operation. The combination of aggression and introversion, in Musek's view leads to a high predisposition to self-aggression - suicide. In 1992, there were 29.5 suicides per 100,000 inhabitants, the second-highest incidence in the world, behind Hungary (39.9) and ahead of Estonia, Finland and Lithuania. There may also be some connection to the large number of traffic accidents, and the high tendency towards alcoholism. Musek, though, reassuringly concludes that 'the unblocking of independence aspirations will diminish the negative and neurotic aspects of the Slovene national character'.

If the national character does improve so much, this 'heaven under Triglav' on the sunny side of the Alps, may prove just too attractive for the tourists it so wants to welcome. The tourists would be torn between staying here forever, or taking a charming Slovene home with them, which would not be good for the country. Researchers at the Statistical Office of the Republic of Slovenia, Vojka Šircelj and Petronela Vertot have data showing that the population of Slovenia will never rise above the two-million mark.

WILL SLOVENES DIE OUT? The population statistics show long-term decline. The average Slovenian woman, with proper male assistance, bears 1.34 children during her lifetime. Leaving aside migration and other factors, this means that by the year 2000 the population would fall by 11,000 to a total of 1,706,000. By 2020 there would be 1,804,000 inhabitants country but only 1,500,000 of them would be ethnic Slovenes. The number of Slovenes would continue to decline and just a few decades later, in 2062, there would be fewer than one million. On this rate, the count-down for the last thousand Slovenes would begin in the year 2435, and take another three centuries. By the year 2745, there would not be a single surviving descendant.

BUT THERE IS STILL HOPE FOR SURVIVAL. The Office of Statistics gives a different, more likely picture. It takes into account that the country is not isolated from the rest of the world and that people will normally migrate in and out. Given past trends, there should be somewhere between 1,998,000 and 2,035,000 inhabitants by the year 2000 and about ten per cent more, 2,207,987 on a high growth variant by the year 2020. There should also be more, not less, ethnic Slovenes.

Blacksmith.

Lepa Vida will be one of them, of course. Hopefully, after all her trials and tribulations she will learn to love life and have more than 1.34 children. She only needs to find a proper partner, and it would even be enjoyable. It is a pity that when Bonaventura Jeglič, Bishop of Ljubljana at the beginning of the century, reiterated the teaching that copulation should only serve for the purpose of procreation, he immediately added: 'It should be done in the early morning hours'.

That is probably where everything went wrong. What could possibly be nicer than sleeping in on a morning?

CHRONOLOGY

AD 44	Start of five centuries of Roman rule over the present territory of Slovenia.
573	First 'Duchy of the Slavs' recorded in a military alliance with the Avars at the eastern end of the Alps.
c. 600	Slav tribes, ancestors of the Slovene people, occupy an area three times the size of Slovenia today.
623	Slavs under King Samo shake off the control of the Avars. Slovene ancestors join this kingdom soon after.
7th c.	Slovene lands known as Karantania, with its centre at Krn Castle, near Klagenfurt.
A.D. 745	Karantania falls under Frankish rule and its inhabitants are gradually converted to Christianity.
Mid 9th c.	Rule of Duke Koceli the last Slovenian duke. Use of the vernacular in Christian liturgy.
1311	Habsburg family acquire their first piece of land beside the River Sava and start expanding the territory under their control towards Carniola.
1408	First Turkish incursions into Slovene territory.
1456	The 'Slovene dynasty' of the counts of Celje dies out.
1479-1490	War between the Hungarians and the Habsburgs. Part of Slovenia occupied by Hungarian King Matthias Corvinus, whose defence of the Slovenes against the Turks wins him a place in Slovene legend.
15th-16th c.	Numerous peasant rebellions against feudal lords and the Church.
1490	Mercury discovered at Idrija.
1515	Peasants' Revolt.
After 1520	First echoes of Protestantism and the Reformation on Slovene soil.
1550	First Slovene books published by Primož Trubar.
1573	Rebellion of Croatian and Slovene peasants led by Matija Gubec cruelly suppressed.
1584	Publication of the first complete Slovene translation of the Bible by Jurij Dalmatin. Adam Bohorič prepares the first Slovene grammar.
1593	Victory over the Ottoman army at Sisak by a joint Carniolan (Slovene) and Croatian force, after which the Turks never enter the area again.
1693	Academia Operosorum Labacensium founded, one of the first scientific institutions in Slovenia.
1701	Academia Philharmonicorum founded, forerunner of the Slovenian Philharmonia.
1719	Trieste and Rijeka (Fiume) become free ports, resulting in increased trade through Slovenia and improvements in communications.
1754	First population census in Slovene regions records 725,000 inhabitants (region east of the River Mura, Istria and the Venetian territories not included).
1770-90	Reforms instituted by Maria Theresa (1717-1793) and Joseph II (1741-1790) introduce compulsory schooling for all, promote religious tolerance, and abolish personal subjection and service to feudal lords.
1789	First stage play written in Slovenian by Anton Tomaž Linhart.
1797	First of two brief invasions by Napoleonic forces.
1797-1800	Valentin Vodnik publishes the first Slovene-language newspaper, *Ljubljanske Novice*.
1809-1813	Napoleon's army occupies the territory of Slovenia. The Illyrian Provinces are established. French role encourages initiatives in the fields of Slovene language and culture and the beginnings of national political activity.
1846	France Prešeren, Slovenia's greatest lyric poet, publishes his anthology *Poezije*.
1846-1857	Graz-Celje-Ljubljana-Trieste railway built, connecting Slovene towns with Vienna and the sea.
1848	'Spring of Nations'. A programme for a united Slovenia drafted, with demands for ethnic and political cohesison, the official recognition of the Slovene languuage, and its own schools and university.
1866	Venetian Slovenes come under Italian rule.
1868-1871	Meetings throughout Slovenia indicate the rise in national consciousness.
1870	Slovene, Croat, and Serbian politicians meet and formulate a joint programme to promote their nationalist and secessionist causes.
1890-91	Foundation of the Catholic and Liberal political movements.

1896	Yugoslav Social-Democratic Party formed, declaring its intention of embarking on a 'collective fight on behalf of all the poor living in the southern Slav lands'.
1915	Italy is promised Trieste, the Slovene coastal territories, Istria and parts of Dalmatia by the secret Treaty of London, in reward for joining the Entente against the Central powers.
1917	Dr Anton Korošec puts forward a demand in the Vienna Parliament for unification of all Slovenes, Croats and Serbs in Austria-Hungary within a single independent state under the Hapsburg crown.
Oct. 1918	An assembly of all South Slavs in the Empire, presided over by Korošec, declares the foundation of the State of Slovenes, Croats and Serbs, and appoints the 'first National Government of Slovenia'.
Dec.1, 1918	Proclamation of the Kingdom of Serbs, Croats and Slovenes.
1920	Italian fascists burn down the Slovene Cultural Centre in Trieste. Some foreign democratic governments take issue with the anti-Slav campaign, but fail to halt the systematic ethnic cleansing and exodus of nearly 100,000 Slovenes.
1928-1929	A Montenegrin deputy shoots the Croatian leader Stjepan Radić and two other Croatian deputies in the Yugoslav Parliament. King Alexander establishes a royal dictatorship, exacerbating relations between Zagreb and Belgrade.
1934	King Alexander assassinated in Marseilles by Croat and Macedonian terrorists working for foreign powers.
1939	Agreement between Zagreb and Belgrade on the creation of the Hrvatska Banovina as the first step towards federalization of Yugoslavia.
March 27, 1941	Military putsch overthrows the government after it signs a pact with the Axis powers.
April 6, 1941	Yugoslavia invaded and defeated by Hitler's forces. Germany, Italy and Hungary divide up Slovenia
April 27, 1941	On the initiative of the Yugoslav communists, a popular front is formed, which after the German attack on the Soviet Union is named the Liberation Front.
May 1941	'Slovene Legion', founded as a secret military force allied to the Slovene Christian Democrats. It eventually fields an army to fight on the side of the German occupiers. (In the period until 1945 the anti-communist Domobran troops twice swear their loyalty to Hitler).
May 3, 1945	Still under German occupation, the 'First Slovene Government' is declared - for the second time.
May 4, 1945	The third 'first Slovene National Government' is declared in the Slovene town of Ajdovščina by the Partisan forces.
May 9, 1945	German and Slovene Domobran troops withdraw from Ljubljana.
1947	The peace treaty established a new border between Italy and Yugoslavia. Trieste is retained by Italy. The definitive border is drawn in October 1954, and forms Slovenia's present-day border with Italy.
June, 1948	Soviet bloc expells Yugoslavia and condemns 'Titoist revisionism'.
1953	Slovene coastal areas and the 'B' zone of the Free Territory of Trieste are returned to Yugoslavia; treaties with Italy are signed.
Early 1970s	Political 'liberals' such as Stane Kavčič, Prime Minister of the Slovenian Government, are forced out of office in all the Yugoslav republics and autonomous provinces.
1974	The new constitution intended to give more rights to the individual Yugoslav republics is not well received amongst Serbian hard-liners.
1980	Death of Josip Broz Tito, followed by the rise of Serbian nationalist and unitarian tendencies.
1986	Memorandum of the Serbian Academy of Sciences and Arts undermines the concept of Yugoslav federalism.
1988	Serbian trade embargo against Slovenia.
1989	Process of political pluralism begins with the formation of the first new political party in Slovenia. The Slovene delegation walks out of an extraordinary congress of the Yugoslav Communist Party in Belgrade. A communist, Milan Kučan, remains President but Slovenia is headed by a Christian Democrat Prime Minister.
Dec.1990	Independence plebiscite held in which 93.2% of the Slovenian electorate vote: 88.2% declare in favour of a sovereign and independent Slovenian state.
June 26-27,1991	Following the declaration of independence, Slovenia is attacked by the Yugoslav Army.
January 15, 1992	Slovenia officially recognized by the European Commission.
May 22, 1992	Slovenia becomes a member of the United Nations.

The photographs in this book have been selected from among 15,000 entries to a national competition, organized by the publishers in conjunction with the Slovenian Tourist Association and Photographers' Association, which was open to both amateurs and professionals.

Atomske Toplice spa, 216, 218;
Joco Balant, 66, 187, 189, 190, 202;
Goran Bertok, 224, 249;
Mirko Bijuklič, 28, 36, 67, 82, 179, 186, 227;
Bruno Bizjak, 45, 174;
Nande Bobič, 238;
Andjeljko Božac, 231, 232;
Darko Bradassi, 7;
Anton Cimprič, 78;
Čateske Toplice spa, 212, 213, 215;
Andrej Družinič, 233;
Marko Feist, 200, 245;
Foto Eka, 188;
Jože Hanc, 70, 76, 81, 132-134, 137-139, 141, 176;
Marjan Humer, 2;
Aleš Fevžar, 199;
Marjan Garbajs, 61, 64, 65, 149, 160, 161, 240, 241;
Bogdan Kladnik, 37, 58, 59, 91, 96-131, 140, 142-144, 146, 150, 153, 155-159, 180, 196, 197, 207, 210, 214;
Stane Klemenc, 5, 23, 24, 33, 53, 56, 73, 79, 85, 89, 90, 145, 167, 172, 191, 217, 221;
Janez Klemenčič, 50, 55, 209;
Edo Kozorog, 18, 252;
Tomaž Kunstelj, 230;
Matevž Lenarčič, 25,
Edi Masnec, 1, 4, 11, 14, 21, 35, 38, 40, 48, 49, 52, 62, 71, 74, 75, 86, 93, 95, 192, 194, 208, 221, 224, 226, 235, 250;
Igor Modic, 3, 8, 16, 20, 44, 47, 51, 60, 83, 154, 201, 205, 206, 222, 223, 225, 234;
Zvone Pelko, 135, 136, 162, 163, 166;
Dr Rafko Podobnik, 92, 168, 203;
Peter Pokorn, 42, 43, 57, 68, 80, 84, 165, 169-171, 173, 175, 184;
Brane Ravnikar, 227;
Janez Skok, 12, 15, 17, 22, 24, 27, 29, 46, 63, 77, 87, 151, 152, 177, 178, 182, 195, 204;
Marko Simić, 229;
Marjan Smerke, 237;
Klara Stanič, 9;
France Stele, 19, 32, 39, 88, 208, 242, 244, 246, 248;
Jože Suhadolnik, 247, 251, 252;
Magda Šturman, 54, 148;
Marko Turk 236;
Zoran Vogrinčič, 198, 219, 220;
Andrej Žigon, 69, 183;
Srdjan Živulović, 6, 193, 239;
Urša Žnidaršič, 185.